Understanding
World History

The Rise
of Islam

Other titles in the series include:
Ancient Chinese Dynasties
Ancient Egypt
Ancient Greece
Ancient Rome
The Black Death
The Decade of the 2000s
The Digital Age
The Early Middle Ages
Elizabethan England
The Enlightenment
The Great Recession
The History of Rock and Roll
The History of Slavery
The Holocaust
The Industrial Revolution
The Late Middle Ages
The Making of the Atomic Bomb
Pearl Harbor
The Renaissance
The Rise of the Nazis
Victorian England

Understanding World History

The Rise of Islam

Toney Allman

Bruno Leone
Series Consultant

ReferencePoint
Press®

San Diego, CA

© 2015 ReferencePoint Press, Inc.
Printed in the United States
For more information, contact:
ReferencePoint Press, Inc.
PO Box 27779
San Diego, CA 92198
www.ReferencePointPress.com

LIBRARY OF CONGRESS CATALOGING-IN-PUBLICATION DATA

Allman, Toney.
  The rise of Islam / By Toney Allman.
    pages cm. -- (Understanding world history series)
  Includes bibliographical references and index.
  ISBN 978-1-60152-744-8 (hardback) -- ISBN 1-60152-744-6 (hardback) 1. Islam--Origin.
2. Islam--History. I. Title.
  BP55.A45   2015
  297.09--dc23
                                                                2014006453

Contents

Foreword

When the Puritans first emigrated from England to America in 1630, they believed that their journey was blessed by a covenant between themselves and God. By the terms of that covenant they agreed to establish a community in the New World dedicated to what they believed was the true Christian faith. God, in turn, would reward their fidelity by making certain that they and their descendants would always experience his protection and enjoy material prosperity. Moreover, the Lord guaranteed that their land would be seen as a shining beacon—or in their words, a "city upon a hill"—that the rest of the world would view with admiration and respect. By embracing this notion that God could and would shower his favor and special blessings upon them, the Puritans were adopting the providential philosophy of history—meaning that history is the unfolding of a plan established or guided by a higher intelligence.

The concept of intercession by a divine power is only one of many explanations of the driving forces of world history. Historians and philosophers alike have subscribed to numerous other ideas. For example, the ancient Greeks and Romans argued that history is cyclical. Nations and civilizations, according to these ancients of the Western world, rise and fall in unpredictable cycles; the only certainty is that these cycles will persist throughout an endless future. The German historian Oswald Spengler (1880–1936) echoed the ancients to some degree in his controversial study *The Decline of the West*. Spengler asserted that all civilizations inevitably pass through stages comparable to the life span of a person: childhood, youth, adulthood, old age, and, eventually, death. As the title of his work implies, Western civilization is currently entering its final stage.

Joining those who see purpose and direction in history are thinkers who completely reject the idea of meaning or certainty. Rather, they reason that since there are far too many random and unseen factors at work on the earth, historians would be unwise to endorse historical predictability of any type. Warfare (both nuclear and conventional), plagues, earthquakes, tsunamis, meteor showers, and other catastrophic world-changing events have loomed large throughout history and prehistory. In his essay "A Free Man's Worship," philosopher and mathematician

Bertrand Russell (1872–1970) supported this argument, which many refer to as the nihilist or chaos theory of history. According to Russell, history follows no preordained path. Rather, the earth itself and all life on earth resulted from, as Russell describes it, an "accidental collocation of atoms." Based on this premise, he pessimistically concluded that all human achievement will eventually be "buried beneath the debris of a universe in ruins."

Whether history does or does not have an underlying purpose, historians, journalists, and countless others have nonetheless left behind a record of human activity tracing back nearly 6,000 years. From the dawn of the great ancient Near Eastern civilizations of Mesopotamia and Egypt to the modern economic and military behemoths China and the United States, humanity's deeds and misdeeds have been and continue to be monitored and recorded. The distinguished British scholar Arnold Toynbee (1889–1975), in his widely acclaimed twelve-volume work entitled *A Study of History*, studied twenty-one different civilizations that have passed through history's pages. He noted with certainty that others would follow.

In the final analysis, the academic and journalistic worlds mostly regard history as a record and explanation of past events. From a more practical perspective, history represents a sequence of building blocks—cultural, technological, military, and political—ready to be utilized and enhanced or maligned and perverted by the present. What that means is that all societies—whether advanced civilizations or preliterate tribal cultures—leave a legacy for succeeding generations to either embrace or disregard.

Recognizing the richness and fullness of history, the ReferencePoint Press Understanding World History series fosters an evaluation and interpretation of history and its influence on later generations. Each volume in the series approaches its subject chronologically and topically, with specific focus on nations, periods, or pivotal events. Primary and secondary source quotations are included, along with complete source notes and suggestions for further research.

Moreover, the series reflects the truism that the key to understanding the present frequently lies in the past. With that in mind, each series title concludes with a legacy chapter that highlights the bonds between past and present and, more important, demonstrates that world history is a continuum of peoples and ideas, sometimes hidden but there nonetheless, waiting to be discovered by those who choose to look.

Important Events During the Rise of Islam

570
The Prophet Muhammad is born in Mecca.

630
Muhammad returns to Mecca, peacefully takes control of the city, and dedicates the Kaaba to Allah. Mecca accepts Islam.

655
Civil war breaks out in Arabia over the right of succession of the caliphate.

622
Muhammad and his followers flee Mecca for Medina. This flight comes to be known as the hegira or migration.

632
Muhammad dies in Medina.

600   **630**   **660**

610
Muhammad receives the first revelation from the angel Gabriel.

634
The establishment of the Islamic Empire begins as Omar, the second patriarchal caliph, launches military campaigns against neighboring empires.

633
Muhammad's successor Abu Bakr puts down the revolt occasioned by Muhammad's death, reunites Arabia, and begins Islamic expansion to the north of Arabia.

661
The Umayyad dynasty begins and moves the capital from Medina to Damascus.

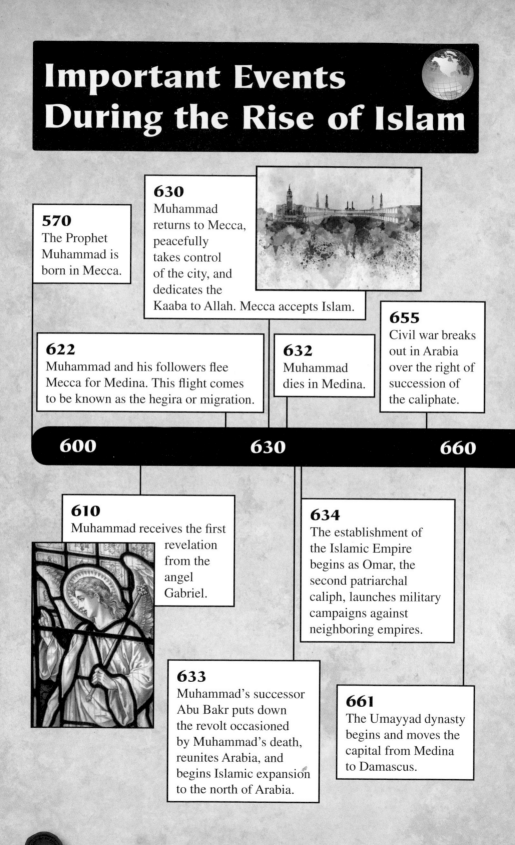

711
The Islamic Empire spreads into Spain and India.

750
The Abbasid dynasty assumes power and moves the capital to Baghdad.

1057
The centralized power of the Islamic Empire begins to shatter as religious differences and the rise of Islamic sects splinter loyalties in the vast empire.

780
Muhammad ibn Musa al-Khwarizmi is born. He will revolutionize mathematics by introducing Arabic numerals to the world and inventing algebra.

1000
Islam spreads through northern and central Africa.

700　　**800**　　**900**　　**1000**

865
Abu Bakr Mohammad Ibn Zakariya al-Razi, the greatest physician of medieval times, is born.

964
The great astronomer Abd-al-Rahman Al Sufi publishes his work *Book of the Fixed Stars*.

c. 768
Historian Ibn Ishaq collects oral histories and records the first biography of Muhammad.

732
The Muslim effort to expand into Europe fails when Muslim armies are stopped in France.

The Defining Characteristics of the Rise of Islam

Perhaps the most defining characteristics of the rise of Islam are its faith-based foundation and the spectacular speed with which its ascent occurred. Islam originated in Arabia, and the religion transformed a primitive, nomadic culture of disunited, often-warring tribes into a cohesive and compelling civilization. The rise of Islam produced an astonishingly sophisticated empire that united vastly disparate peoples and inspired a dynamic growth of human knowledge, creativity, innovation, and social and moral change.

Why Islam?

Islam is first and foremost a religion—the world's youngest major religion—founded by the Prophet Muhammad in the seventh century with the central teaching that there is but one all-powerful, all-knowing God who created the universe. Belief in one God is called monotheism. In the Arabic language, this God is called Allah, but He is the same God worshipped in the other two major monotheistic religions of Christianity and Judaism. Muhammad brought his divinely inspired message of one God before whom every human being is equal to a polytheistic culture dominated by inequality and the belief that tribal leaders and family patriarchs mattered more than ordinary people. (Polytheistic cultures believe in many gods.) The Arabian culture where Islam was born was perhaps perfectly situated to receive and assimilate Muhammad's new religion, but its rapid rise is remarkable. Historian Firas Alkhateeb explains:

> Throughout world history, no other movement has grown as fast as Islam did in its first 100 years. What was special about Islam and the conditions it was born into that allowed it to grow so rapidly? Some historians attempt to offer simplistic explanations about why Islam spread so fast such as drought in the Arabian Peninsula, constant in-fighting among the Arabs, and Arab pride/nationalism. The truth is of course much more complex.[1]

Alkhateeb believes that the conditions that led to Islam's early rapid rise were both geopolitical and cultural. Geopolitically, Arabia was isolated from the rest of Eurasia and never subject to invasion or the domination of empires. Alkhateeb says, "The geographic and thus political isolation of the Arabian Peninsula . . . could not have been more suited for the controversial and radically different message of the Prophet."[2] Culturally, the Arabs were also open to a monotheistic message, says Alkhateeb, because Arab traditions included stories of Abraham and his message of one God from hundreds of years in the past. Miracles were an accepted part of the Arabic polytheistic religion, and so the miracle of Muhammad receiving messages from God was easy to believe. Alkhateeb believes that the perfect conditions for the rise of Islam in Arabia were set up by God in a way that no secular, or nonreligious, historian can understand.

One God, One Community

Whether or not Islam's origins in Arabia were part of a greater plan, it is a fact that by the time of Muhammad's death, all of Arabia had embraced Islam and was unified under the faith and in its belief in Muhammad as leader and God's messenger on earth. The religion had an appeal that was apparently irresistible to a people yearning for hope, meaning, equality, and justice. The Arabian government under Muhammad

An observant Muslim reads the Quran. The Islamic holy book, revealed to Muhammad by God, details each individual's relationship to God as well as how society should function.

was an Islamic government, not a secular one. Muhammad established a society in which Allah was the ultimate authority, and this fusion of religion and government was a unique characteristic of Islam. Every person—regardless of ethnic origin, nationality, class, or race—was bound together by Islam in one community with loyalty to God.

The Islamic holy book, the Quran, revealed to Muhammad by God, not only details each individual's relationship to God but also describes the way society should function and be ruled. Thus, Islam is a universal code of behavior that transcended Muhammad's life, with the Quran and the teachings of Muhammad as guides that future rulers could follow. Faith cemented the people of Arabia into one people with unified goals and inspired their loyalty to their leaders' efforts to expand the influence of Islam, both secularly and religiously. The Quran bade Muslims to wage holy war against those who threatened Islam and to strive to bring the world to God. C. Warren Hollister says, "In the years immediately after Muhammad's death the explosive energy of the Arabs, harnessed at last by the teachings of the Prophet, broke upon the world."[3] Within four decades of the death of Muhammad, Arabia had created a true empire—the Islamic Empire. It not only conquered and ruled territory, nations, and previously powerful empires, it also spread the Muslim faith among millions of converts. Instead of rebellion and resentment, conquered peoples felt allegiance to their new rulers and embraced their new culture and faith.

Faith, Principles, and the Golden Age

Unique among civilizations of the time, the Islamic Empire, in obedience to the Quran, was characterized by tolerance for other religions and cultures, a great respect for learning and knowledge, and an enthusiasm and eagerness to achieve and innovate in every area of life and thought. No one was required to convert to Islam. Conquered peoples were allowed to keep their governments and societies generally intact. The Arabs themselves, dazzled by the riches and luxuries of other cultures, did not destroy but preserved and incorporated the skills required to expand on the wealth they found. When they came across knowledge, invention, or original philosophical thought, they assimilated it, learned from it, made it their own, and improved on it.

The perspectives and attitudes fostered by Islam gave birth to a golden age of civilization that was unparalleled in its contributions to humankind. The Royal Embassy of Saudi Arabia explains:

> Islam fostered the flowering of brilliant civilizations and the development of great centers of learning. It was a period of dynamism, a melding of ancient and new thought, with the Muslim world acting as the repository of knowledge and a bridge between the east and the west. Great contributions were made by Muslim scholars and artists. Islamic civilization—rich, sophisticated and varied—has taken its place among the great cultural achievements of human history.[4]

Chapter 1

What Conditions Led to the Rise of Islam?

In pre-Islamic times, the Arabian Peninsula—where Muhammad lived and the Muslim faith arose—was essentially cut off and isolated from the rest of the world. It was surrounded by mighty empires that vied for power and territory, but because of its forbidding geography, Arabia was not subjected to conquering armies or submission to alien cultures. It was free to develop in its own way. Nevertheless, the course taken by the surrounding civilizations would play an important role in the development of the culture of Arabia and in the eventual rise of Islam.

The Fall of the Roman Empire

Perhaps the event with the biggest impact on the ancient world was the fall of the Roman Empire in 476 CE. At its height, the Roman Empire stretched about 3,000 miles (4,828 km) from west to east, in a crescent around the Mediterranean Sea. It encompassed Greece, North Africa, Egypt, Israel, and Mesopotamia, all the way to the Persian Empire and into Arabia, halted only by the Arabian deserts and the Caucasus Mountains. The realm covered Europe as far north as France and England and stretched up to the territory of the Germanic tribes as well. When the empire began to disintegrate, the effects were felt throughout Eurasia.

By the fifth century, the Roman people and leaders were firmly

Christian, but part of the reason for the empire's demise was that it was so vast as to be uncontrollable from its center. Large areas of the far-flung empire were pagan, polytheistic, or practiced variants of Christianity. Many border areas were subject to constant attacks and invasions from barbarian tribes outside the empire's influence and with different, non-Christian cultures. For example, on the northern borders of the empire, the pagan, barbaric Germanic tribes, known collectively as the Goths, repeatedly invaded western Europe, leading to major disruptions in the culture, war casualties, famines, disease, and population decline.

By the sixth century, the Roman Empire had completely lost control of western Europe and abandoned it. Western Europe, although still mostly Christian, became a wilderness of lost civilization, with primitive, widely scattered villages of subsistence farmers, no cities, loss of knowledge and literacy, and no cohesive structure. Historians Judith M. Bennett and C. Warren Hollister explain that western Europe "fractured into a variety of successor states,"[5] small areas that were controlled by warring, ambitious men who had little success in uniting the many parts of the vast territory. The same fate befell much of North Africa as the barbarian tribe known as the Vandals assailed and conquered this geographical area, ripping it away from the influence and control of the Roman Empire.

The Byzantine and Persian Empires

The eastern half of the Roman Empire survived. Rome was lost, but the embattled survivors of the empire retrenched, with a new, elegant capital known as Constantinople, named in honor of the first Christian emperor, Constantine. It was near an ancient town called Byzantium, and the civilized remnants of the Roman Empire became known as the Byzantine Empire. The empire was powerful and wealthy and, at least for a while, controlled a crescent of geography around the Mediterranean as far as Syria, Palestine, and Egypt. By the early seventh century, however, the Byzantine Empire was shrinking. Bellicose Asian nomads, known as the Avars, captured and subjugated the Slavs and Bulgars of the Balkans. At the same time, the other great empire of the age—the

The prophet Zoroaster founded an ancient monotheistic religion. That religion, known as Zoroastrianism, was the dominant faith of the Persian Empire.

Persian Empire—began to expand and wrested Syria, Egypt, and Palestine from Byzantine control.

The Persian Empire was ruled by the Sassanid dynasty (named for Sassan, the founding ruler's grandfather) from 226 to 651 CE. Like the Byzantine Empire, it was a wealthy and expansionist power, often at war with its neighbors such as the barbarian Huns of Asia and the Byzantines, and it controlled much of the Middle East. Its center and capital were in modern-day Iran. At the height of its power, it included present-day Iran, Iraq, Syria, Lebanon, Palestine, Jordan, Israel, Egypt, and the Caucasus areas of Armenia, Georgia, Dagestan, and Azerbaijan. It also encompassed parts of Turkey, much of Central Asia, the Persian Gulf, and Yemen, Oman, and Pakistan.

The religion of the Sassanids was Zoroastrianism, and its holy books were known as the Avesta. Zoroastrianism was declared the official state religion in the sixth century, and its priesthood was extremely powerful throughout the empire. Zoroastrianism was an ancient religion, even during the Sassanid dynasty. Founded by the prophet Zoroaster (also known as Zarathustra) sometime around 1500 to 1200 BCE, it was—and is today—a monotheistic religion. Zoroastrians believe in one all-wise God (Ahura Mazda) who created the world, and they worship him in a fire temple, not because they are fire worshippers but because they believe that the purity of fire represents God's light and wisdom. Zoroastrianism, along with Christianity, was one of the two most powerful monotheistic religions after the fall of Rome. The other major monotheistic religion was Judaism, but the Hebrew people were scattered throughout Eurasia and had no empire of their own.

The Persian and Byzantine Empires, as well as the various tribes and invaders who controlled smaller territories, were never isolated from one another or even at peace. Christians and Jews lived throughout the Sassanid Empire, and Jews and polytheistic believers lived in the far-flung regions of the Byzantine Empire. All the various societies and cultures battled and invaded one another with regularity—for territory, wealth, and power. All set themselves against those of different religions and believed that they alone followed the correct path. Both the Byzantine and Persian Empires were based on rigid class systems in which the ruling class lived lives of luxury, intellectualism, and grace, while commoners, who were the vast majority of the people, had no education and little to make their lives comfortable. Christian and Zoroastrian priests were wealthy wielders of power and authority who taught that class was dictated by God. All the different cultures held slaves who had no power or rights at all. Rulers periodically sent armies against each other, but as time passed, treaties were agreed on occasionally, oppression of and intolerance for those of different religions were relaxed in some areas, and contact between different cultures became the norm. Trade began to grow in importance as a means of acquiring wealth.

"The Island of the Arabs"

In this world environment of empires, barbarians, and political struggles, Arabia was a place apart. The Arabian Peninsula was an isolated and primitive land. Its civilization lacked the central organization so characteristic of the empires, and its people had never been conquered by outsiders. Both its isolation and its culture were, for the most part, a function of the geography of Arabia, most of which is desert. History professor Firas Alkhateeb explains, "The Arabian Peninsula can be an unforgiving, punishing land. It has no permanent rivers, streams, or lakes. The main source of life are the sparse oases that dot the landscape. Travelling through the desert is a difficult feat to accomplish, and even today there are parts of it that are devoid of any population, due to its lack of water life." The Arabian Peninsula was so forbidding that no foreign army ever succeeded in invading it. Indeed, according to Alkhateeb, the region was known as "the Island of the Arabs."[6]

The Arab culture was tribal, deeply family-oriented, and independent. Most Arabs were Bedouin nomads who traveled the deserts from oasis to oasis with their grazing animals. Most oases are so small that the available animal fodder was quickly depleted, and the nomads were forced to move on to the next oasis just to keep their animals fed. It was an arduous and precarious existence, both for people and animals. Some Bedouins led caravans of camels through the desert—along established traveling routes between oases—and carried goods to trade with the

Beauty Everywhere

Ancient Arab poetry saw beauty everywhere. The Bedouin poet Tarafa lived in the sixth century and was famous for his odes. In this excerpt from one of his odes is his description of his camel:

> Ah, but when grief assails me, straightway I ride it off
> mounted on my swift, lean-flanked camel, night and day
> racing, sure-footed, like the planks of a litter; I urge her
> on down the bright highway, that back of a striped man-
> tle; her long neck is very erect when she lifts it up calling
> to mind the rudder of a Tigris-bound vessel. Her skull is
> most like an anvil, the junction of its two halves meeting
> together as it might be on the edge of a file. Her cheek is
> smooth as Syrian parchment, her split lip a tanned hide
> of Yemen, its slit not bent crooked; her eyes are a pair of
> mirrors, sheltering in the caves of her brow-bones, the
> rock of a pool's hollow. Her trepid heart pulses strongly,
> quick, yet firm as a pounding-rock set in the midst of a
> solid boulder. Such is the beast I ride.

Quoted in *Saudi Aramco World*, "Seven Golden Odes," October 1963, pp. 18–19. www.sau diaramcoworld.com.

several dozen tribes living in the peninsula. Some lived permanently at the few large oases where they had water wells, grew crops, and traded with and offered welcome to visiting nomadic tribes. In their harsh desert lands, survival depended on family or the groups of families that formed clans, because no one could live in the desert alone or without help. Larger tribes formed of several interrelated clans provided kinship protection, too. Allegiance to the family and to the head of the family or tribe was the most important cultural value. Providing needed assistance to a family or clan member and offering hospitality to a stranger in need were also cultural imperatives.

For centuries no central government or government of any kind existed in Arabia. People submitted to the authority of their tribal chiefs—but out of loyalty, not because of laws. When individuals were wronged, they took justice into their own hands and sought the revenge they believed was appropriate. Sometimes family members or the tribe sought justice through a feud or vendetta with the tribe that protected the wrongdoer. Every tribe or clan was equally responsible for the behavior of each of its members under this social system. The right of retaliation for wrongs was called blood vengeance, and every clan or tribe practiced blood vengeance when one of its own was harmed. Historian Lesley Hazleton explains, "If a member of a clan or tribe was killed, then his kin were obliged to seek revenge. Indeed if a man's slaying went unavenged, it was believed that an owl would emerge from his grave calling, 'Give me a drink! Give me a drink!' in demand for blood to slake its thirst."[7]

Intertribal warfare was not uncommon, and enmity between tribes could last for generations. Raiding enemy tribes for goods or killing them to seize their territory was an accepted practice. Disputes were most commonly about water rights, access to grazing for animals, or personal insults or injury to a kinsman. In such a social system, women and girls were of little value, since they could not fight or head and protect a family. The society of the Arabs was so patriarchal that infant boys were prized, but infant girls were often buried alive. Females were considered burdens and had no social status and few rights.

The culture of the Arabs was primitive. They had no written language and little art. Paintings and sculptures were simply impractical, both because nomadic people could not carry superfluous objects through the desert and because the desert provided few natural materials with which to create art. Similarly, the development of architecture was of no use to these nomadic peoples. Their homes were tents or crude dwellings, and there were no kings to create castles or powerful priests to build grand churches. The one exception to this lack of

Bedouin nomads rest at a desert oasis. The Bedouins journeyed from one oasis to another, bringing with them their families, their animals, and goods for trade.

culture was in oral poetry and oration. The Arabic language is flowing and musical, ideally suited to rhymes and rhythms, and the oral art forms flourished. Master poets and wise men composed beautiful poems, histories, and speeches that were memorized and passed down orally through generations. Poets were renowned, and the best of them were celebrated and honored everywhere.

No matter where they lived, the Arabians were closely tied to the natural world and felt a mystical, spiritual connection with nature. They lived in a wilderness, often on the very edge of survival, and their poetry and religion reflected the harsh conditions of their surroundings. They were a polytheistic people who worshipped numerous gods and idols that protected their tribes; controlled the severe weather; ruled the vast night skies, mountains, and sands of the desert; and determined whether the tribe would survive or perish. For hundreds of years, the Arab peoples had little contact with the religious beliefs of others, but by the sixth century, change was coming for some of the large tribes of related clans in the Arabian Peninsula.

Civilization's Inroads

The growth of trade throughout Eurasia brought the Arabs into contact with the outside world. Hollister explains, "A great caravan route running northward from southern Arabia served as an important link in a far-flung commercial network between the Far East and the Byzantine and Persian Empires. Along this route cities developed to serve the caravans, and with city life came a degree of civilization."[8] Leading tribal families formed alliances that controlled the cities that grew up around their oases along the trade route. The most powerful members of these tribes became settled, wealthy merchants and increased their power and influence among the other tribes.

Tribal nomadic life evolved into commercial life for these groups of people. They were exposed to foreigners from other cultures and to the new ideas these people brought with them. The tribes and clans that controlled the cities also controlled the water wells and access to food that grew in the oases. Instead of freely offering welcome and succor to all visitors, as traditions had dictated, the ruling families profited by charging fees for the use of their assets. The Bedouins continued to live as they always had, but the city leaders profited from their outside contacts and became rich.

From Mecca, the biggest and most successful city along the trade route, the ruling tribes sent their own trading caravans throughout the region and into neighboring areas, especially the border areas of the Persian Empire. The city also welcomed visiting trading tribes, as well as travelers who came to visit the most important religious shrine in the Arabian Peninsula—the Kaaba. The Kaaba was a temple dedicated to more than 360 lesser gods, led by the chief god Al-llah, who were worshipped by the tribes of the Arabian Peninsula. Tradition dictated that all tribal fighting cease during pilgrimage season every year so that people could come to the shrine to pray, make offerings, have their fortunes told by magical means, and cleanse themselves of sin. Here the best poets gathered each year to recite their poems. The poems as a whole are called the Mu'allaqat, which means "the suspended." Tradition says the term was used because the best ones were hung, or

Oases

An oasis is a patch of vegetation surrounded by desert and fed by a natural spring or underground water source. Some oases are quite small—no more than a few palm trees growing around a well or spring. Others cover extremely large areas. The Al-Hasa oasis in Arabia, for example, is one of the largest oases in the world. It covers 70 square miles (181 sq. km), holds more than fifty springs, and is suitable for agriculture. The Zamzam spring is the main water source for the city of Mecca, and although the oasis it feeds is not large enough for farming, it covers many acres and led to the establishment of a surrounding city because the well dug over the spring never ran dry.

The oasis of the city of Medina is much larger than that of Mecca. It is fed not only by multiple springs but also by water runoff from the surrounding mountains—enough water to make Medina an agricultural city. In Arabia the most important plant in the oasis was the date palm. Dates were a major food source for people and animals in Arabia, and the trees provided shade and shelter. Arabs called the date palm the "king of the oasis."

suspended, on the walls of the Kaaba when Mecca became a city and its few literate scribes copied them down to be displayed.

At the temple no living thing could be killed, so individuals or clans who were fleeing enemies and feared for their lives could find protection on temple grounds as well. Other people came to swear an oath of faithfulness to each other, solemnly seal deals with each other, or make a vow of blood vengeance. Any commitment of grave importance was best made and settled on the grounds of the Kaaba. The clans that controlled Mecca were the most influential in all of Arabia, in large part because they controlled access to the Kaaba, its mysterious power, and the pilgrimages.

Some Things Change; Some Things Remain the Same

Everyone in Arabia was affected by the trade route and the growth of cities and commercial contacts. Along the main caravan route, markets and fairs were held in the settled cities to which all the tribes came to barter goods, and these gatherings led to cultural exchanges also. People held poetry and oratory contests, swapped stories about their travels, and were introduced to new kinds of tools, clothing, furnishings, and crafts. They were even introduced to money with Byzantine solidus and Sassanid drachmas.

The nomadic Bedouins traded olive oil, wool, leather bags, and water jugs for food, clothing, and pots and pans, but many did more than trade. As the caravans passed along the trading route, the Bedouins frequently attacked them and seized all their camels and the trading goods. Sometimes they also kidnapped women and children and held them for ransom. Naturally, this meant that the settled merchants had to hire other Bedouins for protection for their caravans. Historian Nihal Sahin Utku says:

> During this period, the Bedouins delivered goods to fairs organized in various locations of the peninsula, becoming experts in the caravan trade. Soon the Bedouins provided camels for the international trade caravans that started their journeys in India and China and went as far as Egypt and the Mediterranean Sea through Yemen and the Red Sea. In addition to this, they also maintained the safety of the caravan routes and protected them from various attacks. The income obtained from caravan protection and services as guides for travelers and trade convoys passing through their lands constituted a significant income.[9]

The world was opening up for the Arabs, and they eagerly grasped at the potential benefits while fiercely fighting to maintain their own values and way of life. The settled tribes in the cities learned the comforts of a new way of life, but they clung to their Bedouin roots by

The most important religious shrine on the Arabian Peninsula, the Kaaba (pictured), provided a place for prayer and for securing important commitments. The temple grounds also provided safe haven from warring clans.

maintaining a reverence for the nomadic culture that seemed to them pure, noble, and honorable. The leading tribes also maintained their own beliefs in the importance of kinship ties. They established no city governments but ruled through consensus among clan leaders. The Bedouins themselves participated in the caravan trade while holding themselves and their values apart from it. They disdained the cities except for visits and kept to their traditional ways.

The introduction to civilization brought disruption for many and yet did little to change the inequities of the culture. As with the empires, the ruling classes found luxuries and comforts while the vast majority of the people suffered or barely survived. Lawlessness abounded. Slaves and women were powerless. And in this patriarchal culture, children were defenseless without a father or male kinsman to protect and support them. Dissatisfaction with social norms increased as people came into contact with other cultures. Inequality and injustice were rampant. To modern Muslims, this time is known as the "Age of Ignorance."[10]

At a Critical Point in a Critical Time

In the late sixth and early seventh centuries, the Arabs were a people awakening to the larger world that encompassed them and eager to take advantage of expanding opportunities, yet they were fervently proud of their own culture and independence. They remained tribal and polytheistic, an insignificant political force surrounded by great empires. But the Arab culture was in transition; its awareness of possibilities was growing. At the same time, the Byzantine and Persian Empires were economically, politically, and militarily weakening from years of warfare and expansionist policies. Into this developing, evolving environment the Prophet Muhammad was born, in the thriving city of Mecca. His new religion would revolutionize the world.

Chapter 2

Born into a Changing World

Muhammad, the founder of Islam, is such a legendary and revered figure that it can be difficult to reconcile the varying accounts and interpretations of his life and personality. Most information about him comes from two early biographers, who wrote at least a century after Muhammad's death. In the eighth century a Syrian named Ibn Ishaq wrote a lengthy account of Muhammad's life, and in the ninth century a historian in Baghdad named al-Tabari wrote a multivolume history of Islam that included four volumes describing Muhammad's life. These two biographers tried to include every detail known or reported to them, but even they sometimes wrote that they could not be sure of the accuracy of the details in the oral histories they were recording. Modern historians depend heavily on the works of these men, but no one can be sure that every anecdote is the truth. Nevertheless, understanding Islam and its rise means trying to understand the man who was the first Muslim and how he himself rose from obscurity to establish one of the world's greatest religions.

A Precarious Beginning

Muhammad was born in Mecca around 571 CE, under conditions that did not bode well for his survival. Muhammad's grandfather, Abd al-Muttalib, was the leader of the Hashim clan. This clan was one of the four major clans that had banded together to form the powerful Quraysh tribe that controlled Mecca. Abd al-Muttalib's favorite son

A Marriage Proposal

Muhammad was too young and humble to propose marriage to a woman as wealthy and important as Khadija. Instead, she proposed to him. She wanted to marry him but was unsure of herself because he was so much younger. Perhaps he would not be interested. She sent a friend named Nufaysah to find out how Muhammad felt about her. Nufaysah asked Muhammad why he had not married, and he told her he did not have enough money to marry anyone. She replied, "But if thou wert given the means and if thou wert bidden to an alliance where there is beauty and property and nobility and abundance, wouldst thou not consent?" Muhammad asked who that woman could be, and when Nufaysah said it was Khadija, he asked, "And how could such a marriage be mine?" Nufaysah replied, "Leave that to me!" And Muhammad answered, "For my part, I am willing."

Nufaysah went back to Khadija and reported on the conversation. Then Khadija invited Muhammad to come talk to her in person. She proposed to him during the visit, and he accepted. As was the Arabian tradition, relatives of both of them made the formal arrangements for the wedding. The parties agreed that Muhammad would be the one to bring a dowry to the marriage. Twenty female camels were agreed on as Muhammad's marriage gift to his bride.

Quoted in Martin Lings, "Prophet Muhammad's First Marriage," Tell Me About Islam, 2013. www.tellmeaboutislam.com.

was Abdullah, who was a trade caravan leader. Abdullah married a woman named Amina, and just three days after the wedding, he left with a trade caravan to journey to the city of Damascus. It was a long, difficult trek, and accidents or sickness were common killers of caravan members. On the way home from Damascus, in a stopover in the Arabian city of Medina, Abdullah died, never knowing that his new wife was pregnant with his son, whom she would name Muhammad. Thus, Muhammad may have had distinguished roots, but he was born effectively an orphan. Lesley Hazleton says, "In a society that venerated fathers, he was born without one. And sixth-century Mecca was not kind to either widows or orphans."[11]

According to tribal law, only an adult son could inherit anything after a father's death. If a woman was left a widow or a son lost his father before he was grown, the inheritance passed to an adult male relative such as a brother, uncle, or cousin. This male relative was then supposed to take on the responsibility of the dead man's family. Abdullah's father, Abd al-Muttalib, inherited Abdullah's estate, but in the changing environment of Mecca, where tribal responsibilities were often neglected, the old man had little or no interest in his son's wife of a few days and her newborn baby. They were penniless, unwanted, and ignored.

Like every city in the ancient world, Mecca was not a healthy environment for infants. Infant mortality due to disease and malnutrition was high, and well-born women in Mecca usually sent their infants to Bedouin wet nurses and the healthier environment of the desert for the first two years of the baby's life. This practice increased infants' chances of survival. Bedouin women with infants earned money for their tribes by taking on the job of nursing the child of a wealthy family along with their own babies.

Usually, Meccan women hired healthy Bedouin women from well-off nomadic tribes, but Amina had no money to pay a wet nurse. She could find no one to take her infant until a poor, half-starved, desperate Bedouin woman from a tribe barely surviving a terrible periodic drought rode into the city on a weak, starving donkey. This woman, Halima, needed an infant to foster, but wealthy women would pay only for a healthy woman, and Amina could not pay at all. At first, according to the old accounts, Halima refused Amina's baby, but no one else would hire her. Then, she explained years later, "when we decided to depart [from Mecca], I said to my husband, 'By God, I do not like the idea of returning without a suckling. I will go and take that orphan.' . . . So I went back and took him for the sole reason that I could not find any other infant."[12]

An Orphan's Hard Childhood

So it happened that Muhammad spent his first five years living the life of a nomadic Bedouin child. No one knows for sure why he was not returned to his mother when he was weaned, but some historians speculate that she never sent for him because she could not afford to raise him or pay his foster family for his care. So Halima and her family kept him. Muhammad and his foster family and tribe were poor and struggled to survive in the harsh desert, but Muhammad learned the skills and values that had served the Arabs well for hundreds of years. Even at this young age, he worked with his foster brother and sisters like a typical Bedouin child. He helped herd the tribe's flocks of grazing sheep, learned to handle the goats and camels, took the animals to the wells to drink, and guarded the flocks at night from the hyenas and mountain lions that preyed on them. He learned to love the freedom to roam in the open spaces of his land, recognize the beauty and purity of the vast desert, and appreciate the wonders of nature. Yet always he was reminded that he did not truly belong. The tribe called him "the Qurayshi,"[13] after the tribe to which he was born.

When Muhammad was five years old, Halima and her family returned him to his mother in Mecca, but the reunion did not last long. When Muhammad was six, Amina took him on a trip to Medina, 200 miles (322 km) north of Mecca, so he could visit his father's grave. On the return trip, Amina fell ill with a fever and died. Muhammad was now twice an orphan, and his grandfather took over his care. Abd al-Muttalib, however, was eighty years old and ill, and his power in Mecca was waning. His Hashim clan was losing influence, and the influence of the Umayyad clan was growing in the Quraysh tribe. Some historians believe that Muhammad became his grandfather's favorite, but others suggest that the boy was basically ignored. Whatever the truth, this relationship was short lived, too. When Muhammad was eight,

The caravan trader, Abu Talib, took the young Muhammad into his care. Under Talib's guidance, Muhammad worked as a camel boy— guiding, feeding, and generally caring for the trader's valuable camels.

his grandfather died, and his uncle, Abu Talib, became the head of the Hashim clan and took Muhammad into his household.

Abu Talib was a caravan trader, but he was not wealthy and had a large family to support. Muhammad was put to work as a camel boy, and his early experiences in the desert made him good at the job. He handled the cantankerous animals with skill, and within two years the boy was accompanying his uncle on trading missions. As one of the camel boys, Muhammad walked beside and guided the camels during the treks, fed and watered them at the end of each day, collected their dung for fuel for cooking fires, and tethered and guarded the camels from predators every night. In addition, he was responsible for making sure the caravan merchants were comfortable. They rode instead of walking and expected the camel boys to fetch their water, bring them their meals, and wait on them whenever they commanded. It was hard work, but Muhammad proved himself reliable and trustworthy, and his uncle came to depend on him as an essential member of the caravan journeys.

During one long trading trip to Syria, when Muhammad was ten or twelve years old, Ibn Ishaq recounts that Muhammad was the subject of an amazing prophecy. The caravan route passed close by an isolated monastery where a solitary Christian monk named Bahira lived. Bahira invited the caravan members to stop and rest at his monastery. When he saw Muhammad, the monk felt that he was looking at a boy who would be a great prophet someday. He examined the child and is said to have found a mark on his back, between the shoulder blades; this mark, according to Bahira's holy book (perhaps an ancient copy of the Bible), was a sign of a prophet.

The Arabians were illiterate, but they had a great reverence for cultures and people who actually had books. Indeed, they referred to Christians and Jews as the People of the Book, who were powerful because their God gave them a holy book. According to a historical website about Islam's holy places, Bahira said to the Arabian travelers, "This is the master of all humans, Allah will send him with a message which would be a mercy to all humans."[14] Perhaps the assembly believed the truth of this prophecy because Bahira said it was from the book, or perhaps they thought Bahira had lost his senses in the heat and loneliness of the desert. However Muhammad and his uncle reacted to the monk's words, the prophecy did not seem to change Muhammad's day-to-day life.

Young Adulthood

Muhammad spent his childhood and adolescence working in the caravan trade for his uncle and taking on more and more responsibility. By watching his uncle, he learned how to be a successful caravan trader. A caravan trek was a complex undertaking that could last for months. At oasis stops along the way to their destination, Muhammad learned the diplomacy that was so important for a successful journey. They made friends with the clans at each stop, sharing meals and hospitality with graciousness. At their destination, they carefully negotiated to get the best deals for their goods, and that meant knowing the value of the goods they carried. Then, when the caravan arrived home, the earned profits had to be distributed fairly among all the participating

During the time that Muhammad was growing up in Mecca, the Kaaba was a relatively small, cubic structure with walls made of stone and clay and a roof of palm fronds and cloth. It was just tall enough for a person to enter through its low doorway. Tradition had it that the Kaaba was first built as a shrine or tabernacle by the prophet Abraham and his son Ishmael. It was built in a hollow in the city, between wadis—dry riverbeds that held water only during the rare heavy rains that flooded the area. Around the Kaaba stood idols of uncarved stones—historians disagree about the number—where people made sacrifices and gave offerings. Usually, historians say that three of the stones represented the three daughters of Al-llah—Manat, Lat, and Uzza. Inside the Kaaba, different historians describe different things. Some say there were only the horns of a ram; others insist there were idols for every tribe in Arabia. All historians agree, however, that in one corner sat the Black Stone, which Muslim tradition says is a meteorite that dates to the time of Adam and Eve. It was a sacred stone, even in pre-Islamic times, but later both the Black Stone and the Kaaba itself would be dedicated to Islam and God.

merchants who had sent goods for trade. Arguments about the amount of profit due each of several merchants were frequent. Suspicions that caravan leaders kept unreported profits for themselves were common. The honest caravan leader knew how to establish confidence in his dealings and negotiate a fair percentage of the profits for everyone. Muhammad learned all these skills and became his uncle's second in command.

By the time Muhammad was twenty-five years old, he had become a skilled, capable, and trustworthy caravan leader. He remained unschooled and illiterate, but he gained a meaningful education in his constant travels. He was exposed to many different religions and cultures. He met Christians, Jews, Zoroastrians, and Hindus, learned of their sacred books, became familiar with different systems of government, and observed how various belief systems did and did not affect cultures and morality. He also learned to be an excellent businessman and to secure good profits for his uncle. He had grown into an honest, thoughtful, kindhearted, and intelligent man.

Marriage

Then Muhammad asked Abu Talib for permission to marry his daughter Fakhita. It was not a marriage for love that he asked for, but an alliance that would seal Muhammad's position as a true member of the family and a man as close as a son to Abu Talib, instead of the poor orphan he had always been. Abu Talib rejected the request. His daughter would marry one of the elites of Mecca, an aristocrat, not a man with no father and no inheritance. Abu Talib arranged such a marriage for Fakhita soon after refusing Muhammad's request. Hazleton says that the message to

A Muslim couple weds. Muhammad prospered after his marriage to Khadija, a merchant woman from Mecca. The couple chose to live simply, spurning the luxuries of the wealthy and rejecting society's inequities.

Muhammad was "good but not good enough." She says, "In his uncle's mind, Muhammad was still 'one of us, yet not one of us.'"[15]

The incident was a blow, and Muhammad decided to leave his uncle's household and strike out on his own. He went to work as a caravan leader and business manager for a wealthy Meccan merchant woman named Khadija. She was forty years old, twice a widow, and a member of the powerful Asad clan. Khadija was impressed by Muhammad's honesty, gentleness, and kindness, as well as his business skills. As time went on, the two fell in love and married, despite the difference in their ages.

Now, for the first time, Muhammad's life situation was prosperous and comfortable. The marriage brought him financial security and social respect, but it was also a true love match. In a society in which men usually had several wives, Muhammad remained faithful to Khadija and took no other wives for twenty-four years—until Khadija's death. By the time he was in his thirties, Muhammad and Khadija had four daughters, as well as one son who died in infancy. Muhammad was also raising Ali, the youngest son of his uncle Abu Talib, who had fallen on hard times. Muhammad had freed and adopted a slave boy, Zayd, given to him by Khadija at their marriage, and was raising the child as his own. The family was happy and well off, but by preference they lived a simple life, spurning the luxuries of the wealthy and rejecting the inequities of Meccan society.

A Caring and Sensitive Man

By all accounts, Muhammad recognized and was disturbed by the many cruelties and injustices in Arabic society and in the more sophisticated world outside. He seemed to see clearly how the rich and powerful always prevailed while the poor and powerless suffered and never bettered their lot, despite the teachings of love, equality, and peace among the major monotheistic religions. The pagan religious practices of Arabia did not even pretend to offer comfort to or concern about the have-nots of the society.

Religious writer Mirza Bashiruddin Mahmud Ahmad says of Muhammad, "From very childhood he was given to reflection and meditation."[16] Ahmad describes Muhammad as a sensitive and spiritual man who believed in fairness, equal justice for everyone, kind treatment of slaves, respect for women, and caring for the poor. He not only refused to own slaves but also gave away to the poor any bonuses or commissions he earned in his trading missions. He insisted on living a simple life. He dressed in plain, homemade linen clothing instead of the silks and imported clothing that other wealthy people chose. He ate simple foods instead of indulging in rich feasts. His home was furnished comfortably but not luxuriously. At the Kaaba temple, other men gathered to party, drink, and gamble and sought to make a profit off visiting pilgrims. Muhammad preferred to meditate alone.

Muhammad often retreated to the desert and mountains surrounding Mecca so as to be alone and meditate and to look for a higher meaning and understanding of life. It was during one of these retreats, when he was forty years old, that he had a mystical experience that changed his life—and eventually, the world.

The First Revelation

In about 610 CE, Muhammad went on a retreat to Mount Hira (also known today as Jabal-al-Nour, or Mountain of Light), a rocky hillside where he could find refuge in a small cave. The biographer Ibn Ishaq describes the vision that happened one night during this retreat:

In the night the angel Gabriel came with the command of Allah. The apostle of Allah [Muhammad] later said, "He came while I was asleep, with a cloth of brocade whereon there was writing, and he said, 'Read.' I replied, 'I cannot read it.' Then he pressed the cloth on me till I thought I was dying; he released his hold and said, 'Read.' I replied, 'I cannot read it.' And he pressed me again with it, till I thought I was dying. Then he loosed his hold of me and said, 'Read.' I replied, 'I cannot read it.' Once more he pressed me and said, 'Read.' Then I asked, 'What shall I read?' And I said this because I feared he would press me again. Then he said, 'Read in the name of the Lord thy creator; who created man from a drop of blood. Read, thy Lord is the most bountiful, who taught by means of the pen, taught man what he knew not.' Accordingly I read these words, and he had finished his task and departed from me. I awoke from my sleep, and felt as if words had been graven on my heart."[17]

Muhammad was terrified by his vision. He later said to a follower about the experience:

There was none of God's creation more hateful to me than a poet or a madman; I could not bear to look at either of them, yet I thought, "I must be either a poet or a madman. . . . I shall take myself to a mountain cliff, hurl myself down from it, and find respite in death." But when I came near the top of the mountain I heard a voice from heaven saying, "Muhammad, you are the messenger of God." I raised my head to see who was speaking and there Gabriel was in the form of a man with feet astride the horizon.[18]

The angel stopped Muhammad from committing suicide, but he was still shocked and horrified by what seemed to be happening to him. He could not believe it was real. Sweating and shivering, he ran down the mountain and home to Khadija.

Muhammad threw himself at Khadija's feet, his head in her lap, and begged her to hide him and comfort him. All night Khadija cradled her husband in her arms and covered him with a blanket because he was so cold. As he told her the story of his experience, he repeated perfectly the words that Gabriel had ordered him to read (or recite, as it is sometimes translated). Khadija had never heard Muhammad speak in such a beautiful way before. She believed what had happened to Muhammad was a real holy vision and that the recitation he spoke was truly given to him by God. Muhammad told her that he must now be insane or perhaps tricked by an evil jinn (spirit), but Khadija reassured him that God would never punish such a good man as he with madness. She insisted that God would never abandon him and that instead, he had been chosen for some true and sacred reason.

In the morning, when Muhammad had finally fallen asleep, Khadija walked to her cousin Waraqa's house to ask his advice. Waraqa was an elderly man who had become a Christian and who read the Christian Gospels and the Torah of the Jews. He told Khadija that Muhammad had been visited by the same angel Gabriel who had appeared to Moses long ago. Moses was the prophet of the Jewish people, and Muhammad—if the experience was real—was the messenger for the Arabs. The one almighty God, who in Arabic was known as Allah, had chosen him. According to Ibn Ishaq, Waraqa proclaimed, "Holy! Holy! Verily by Him in whose hand is Waraqa's soul, if thou has spoken to me the truth . . . he is the prophet of his people."[19]

Khadija returned home, sure that their lives had changed forever and that Muhammad now had a special purpose. When Muhammad awoke, she told him all that Waraqa had said. Still frightened and unsure, Muhammad met with Waraqa at the Kaaba. The old man reassured Muhammad again, saying, "In the name of the God who is in control of my life, you are the prophet of this Arabic nation and you received the great signs from God who came to Moses in time past. People will deny you and persecute you and kick you out of your city and fight you and if I am alive when that time comes, I will defend Allah in the way no one can know except Allah himself."[20]

Acceptance

Waraqa and Khadija were the first believers in Muhammad's message and his mission, but Waraqa was not able to keep his promise to speak for and stand up for Muhammad. He died just a few days after the two met at the Kaaba. Khadija was Muhammad's sole support in the days after the first revelation. Her steadfast faith in him helped Muhammad come to terms with the vision and the words he had been given. He began to accept that his experience with the angel Gabriel had given him a true message from Allah. He began to prepare himself to do Allah's will. Muhammad now had a holy mission, and he would do his best to live up to Allah's command.

Chapter 3

Muhammad's Faith

Muhammad's first revelation became the first of the verses that would eventually make up the Quran—the Muslim holy book—although at first the verses would be memorized and passed on only orally in this mostly illiterate Arabian society. *Quran* means "reading" or "recitation," and the Quran is a compilation of all the recitations given to Muhammad by Allah, with the verses organized into chapters called suras. The suras are not in chronological order, but each is considered a recitation of the literal word of God, as given to Muhammad and arranged in the order dictated by him. In all, throughout his lifetime, Muhammad received revelations that make up 114 suras, but in the months following his first revelation, he had no idea of what the future would bring. The tenets of Muhammad's faith grew slowly. Muhammad's religion of Islam, which means "submission," developed as he received further revelations from Allah. From the beginning, however, Muhammad submitted himself completely to God.

The Testing of Faith

For two years after the first revelation on Mount Hira, Muhammad had no more visions or revelations. It was a terrible and lonely time for him. He struggled with doubt, wondering what the silence meant. He had accepted his experience and submitted to God, but now he questioned himself and worried that he had done something that had displeased God. He could not bring himself to keep working as a caravan trader.

Instead, he regularly returned to Mount Hira for retreats and meditation and tried to figure out if God had abandoned him. Finally, the time came when the Voice he longed to hear spoke to him again—a time that is called in the Quran the Sura of the Morning. Ibn Ishaq records the verses of that revelation:

> By brightness, and by the night when it is dark, thy Lord has not forsaken nor hated thee, and the next life will be better for thee than the first. The Lord will give thee victory in this world and reward in the next. Did He not find thee an orphan and procure thee shelter? He found thee erring and guided thee; He found thee needy and enriched thee. Declare the goodness of thy Lord; declare what has come to thee from Allah, and declare His bounty and grace in thy mission; mention it, record it, and pray for manifestations of it.[21]

Now, Muhammad's mission was clear. He was to declare—to spread Allah's message to others, to record the verses he was given, and to pray. Ibn Ishaq explains, "Accordingly the apostle of Allah began, at first in secret to those of his family whom he trusted, to promulgate the gospel bestowed by Allah on him, and on mankind through his agency."[22] Many more revelations followed, often without warning, and they were beautiful, poetic verses that clarified God's messages. Muhammad never knew when or where a new vision would come, but each left him shaking, weak, and exhausted, even though he felt inspired and blessed.

The Mission Begins

In the beginning Muhammad told only his wife the words of each new revelation. Khadija was the first believer in the new religion of Islam and in Muhammad as its prophet—the speaker of God's will through divine inspiration. After some months of visions, the Voice told Muhammad to prepare a dinner of wheat, mutton, and milk and to invite his relatives of the Hashim clan to the meal. Then, he was told, he should recite to these clan members all the words he had been given so far. Forty men came to the feast, including Muhammad's uncle Abu Talib. After dinner Muhammad began to declare the verses to them all. Most were stunned and amazed to hear Muhammad speak so eloquently and poetically, but one, an uncle named Abu Lahab, was outraged. He angrily left the house and refused to listen. The meeting broke up in confusion. Undeterred, Muhammad invited them all back for another meal the next evening. Abu Lahab did not come, but the others stayed to listen to the rest of the recitations. Then Muhammad said to them, "Sons of Abd al-Muttalib, I know of no man among the Arabs who has brought his people something better than what I have brought you. I bring you the best of this world and the next, for God has commanded me to summon you to him. Which of you will aid me in this matter?"[23]

No one responded to Muhammad's plea except Ali, the son of Muhammad's uncle Abu Talib who had been adopted by Muhammad and

Muhammad regularly returned to Mount Hira (pictured in more recent times) to meditate. There, once again, he had a revelation: His mission was to spread God's message to others.

was still a child. The rest of the men left, laughing at Muhammad and confused by his strange claims of receiving visions from God. Ali became the first child to accept Islam and to believe that Muhammad was the true messenger of God. Then other young people of the Hashim clan came to hear more of Muhammad's religion and pray with him and Ali. Zayd, the slave boy freed and adopted by Muhammad, joined them. Muhammad's good friend, a merchant named Abu Bakr, heard Muhammad's message and became the first man to accept Islam. A handful of Abu Bakr's friends joined with them as well. In the first few years after the first revelation, these few men and Khadija were the only believers in Islam and Muhammad.

For their time and their culture, their religion was radical. They professed that Allah is the one all-powerful, all-knowing, all-merciful God. They prayed, as God had told Muhammad to pray, to the one, true God. It was the same God who had spoken to Moses and the Jews and then to Jesus and the Christians. Moses and Jesus were God's prophets, but their message had been corrupted by people over time. Now Muhammad was the prophet of the Arabs, and he was the last prophet because his revelations came from God's holy book and were uncorrupted and pure. The faithful few believed that Muhammad was the apostle and prophet of Allah and that Muhammad's revelations were the true words of God. They were Muslims—those who surrendered to Allah.

Going Public with the Mission

At last Muhammad was commanded to speak publicly and condemn the idols at the Kaaba. The Saudi Arabian website, The Religion of Islam, explains:

> At the end of the third year, the Prophet received the command to "arise and warn," whereupon he began to preach in public, pointing out the wretched folly of idolatry in face of the marvelous laws of day and night, of life and death, of growth and decay, which manifest the power of God and attest to His Oneness.

It was then, when he began to speak against their gods, that Qureysh became actively hostile, persecuting his poorer disciples, mocking and insulting him.[24]

The verses that Muhammad preached in public were almost political as well as religious because they attacked and criticized the social structure and culture of Mecca and all of Arabia. Muhammad not only condemned the worship of idols at the Kaaba, which had made Mecca wealthy, he also condemned the pursuit of wealth at the expense of the poor. The verses he spoke said that the oppressed people—such as slaves, the poor, and abused women—were the true inheritors of

A Persecuted Disciple

One of the first converts to the new religion of Islam was a black slave named Bilal. Bilal's owner, Umayyah ibn Khalaf, was furious with his slave and tortured him for his faith. Umayyah beat Bilal, dragged him into the desert by his neck, threw him on his back, and placed a huge rock on his chest. He told Bilal to renounce Islam and Muhammad or die. This treatment was repeated day after day, but all Bilal would say, according to Muhammad's early biographer Ibn Ishaq, was "One God! One!" One day, Muhammad's good friend Abu Bakr came on the scene of Bilal's torture. Abu Bakr was horrified and persuaded Umayyah to sell Bilal to him. Abu Bakr took Bilal home, cared for him until he recovered, and then freed him. Bilal became a close companion of Muhammad and spent the rest of his life living by his side and took on the duty of waking Muhammad each morning.

Quoted in Ibn Ishaq, *Sirat Rasoul Allah*, Internet Archive, p. 27. https://archive.org.

the earth and of God's blessings. They condemned valuing sons over daughters and the practice of female infanticide as against God. The verses proclaimed that all were equal and equally deserving and worthwhile to God. The clan elders were no more important than youths, widows, orphans, or slaves. Nobles were no better than the poorest free men. Muhammad's preaching was a passionate call for justice. Hazleton says the elders and rulers of the clans of Mecca were furious and determined to stop this "nobody," this "rabble-rouser"[25] who dared to threaten their way of life.

Grief and Persecution

All of Mecca was talking about the new religion, and the Meccan leaders were determined to put a stop to Muhammad's teachings. People took sides for or against Muhammad, and a few more—even well-born ones—began to believe. Then tragedy struck. In about 620 CE, Khadija suddenly died. Muhammad was grief stricken; he had lost the woman who was his closest confidante and who had believed in him from the beginning. Then a few months later, Abu Talib became ill and died as well. Although he had not believed in Islam, Abu Talib had defended and stood by his nephew. Now Muhammad had lost the love and protection on which he had depended. Muhammad's uncle Abu Lahab, his fierce opponent, became the head of the Hashim clan. Abu Lahab withdrew the clan's protection from Muhammad. This meant that, by the honor code of the Arabs, if anyone attacked Muhammad, the clan would not seek revenge.

At first the attacks mounted against Muhammad were more humiliating than life threatening. Someone dumped a pail of dust on his head; someone else threw stones at him as he walked by on the street; someone threw the innards of a slaughtered sheep on him, splattering him with guts and blood. At last, however, the Quraysh leaders plotted to murder Muhammad and destroy his followers. Muhammad decided that they must all flee Mecca for Medina, where they had friends who would offer them sanctuary. In secrecy and small groups of two or three, the Muslim believers sneaked out of the city to travel to Medina.

Muhammad had endured all the persecutions peacefully, but during this time, God gave him the revelation known as the Pledge of War. The verses say:

> Permission is given unto those who fight because they have been wronged, and God is indeed able to give them victory; those who have been driven from their homes unjustly only because they said—Our Lord is God! For were it not that God repels some people by means of others, monasteries and churches and synagogues and mosques in which the name of God is extolled would surely have been destroyed.[26]

In Medina

In 622 CE Muhammad, along with Abu Bakr and their families, left Mecca, ready to fight for their religion and God if need be. The migration from Mecca to Medina is known as the hegira—the flight. Muhammad and his community of Muslims were welcomed in Medina, and Muhammad's first act was to build the first mosque there, where Muslims could worship and pray together in the open and without fear. Muhammad built a compound of small, simple houses for himself, his family, and some of his close followers next to the mosque. Many of the Arabs of Medina converted to Islam, and the Jewish and Christian communities living in Medina welcomed the Muslims as allies who believed in the one God. For the next eight years, Muhammad lived in Medina, uniting the various clans and tribes in the area and bringing peace to a city and its surroundings that had long known only feuds and dissension.

With his ability to resolve disputes and unite people, Muhammad quickly became the leader of Medina, both religiously and politically. He was no longer just a preacher, but a reformer and a lawgiver. Civil and religious authority were fused under Muhammad and directed by the Voice of God. Muhammad established what was almost a constitution for his people that laid out their rights and responsibilities in the new society. God and the revelations helped Muhammad develop

A hadith is a saying or action of Muhammad. During his lifetime Muhammad did not want his words or actions to be recorded, and he disapproved of the practice. He was concerned that such writings would be confused with the perfect words of the Quran that came from God. Nevertheless, some people began writing down his deeds anyway and recording his words. Others simply told friends or family members something that Muhammad had said or done. In the decades after Muhammad's death, the hadith literature was collected and structured by followers, religious experts, and legal authorities and became second only to the Quran as a moral and religious guide for Muslims. Different hadith collections exist today in the Muslim world, but all purport to have come originally from people close to Muhammad, passed down orally or in writing over centuries. One of the most respected collections of hadiths was compiled by Imam Muhammad al-Bukhari in 870 CE. An example of a saying he reports is, "The Prophet said, 'The one who looks after a widow or a poor person is like a Mujahid (warrior) who fights for Allah's Cause, or like him who performs prayers all the night and fasts all the day.'"

Quoted in Sunnah.com, "69: Supporting the Family." http://sunnah.com.

Islamic law and make the right decisions. He would meditate and the Voice would come to him.

Under Islam and Muhammad, the people of Medina became prosperous and strong, but not everyone accepted Islam or Muhammad's authority. Some only pretended to accept Islam, and they became known to the Muslims as the hypocrites. Some, especially of the surrounding

Bedouin tribes, refused to acknowledge Muhammad's right to leadership. The three Jewish tribes in Medina originally signed a pact with the Muslims in which all agreed to defend and honor each other as the People of the Book, but as time passed and Muhammad developed more and more Islamic laws, the Jews resisted.

Holy Armies for Islam

Muhammad felt betrayed by the Jewish rejection of Islam. They were unbelievers who opposed the one true religion revealed by Allah. He and his followers also felt anger and betrayal about the years of bad treatment in Mecca and their ultimate exile. God had said that they could fight against those who wronged them, so the Muslims began harassing Meccan caravans with raids. By 624 the raiding escalated into sporadic battles between small Muslim armies and Meccan armies protecting the larger caravans. The Meccans attempted to conquer Medina itself but failed, and the Muslims knew that they were victorious because God was on their side. Muhammad then sent out armies to the Bedouins in the region. The armies were to fight those who refused to join with Medina against their enemies. Many of the Bedouin tribes joined with Muhammad's followers and accepted Islam.

Muhammad believed that the three Jewish tribes of Medina were aiding the Meccans against him. First he ordered that two of the tribes be expelled from Medina on the charge of disloyalty. Muhammad's revelations supported this action against the Jews of Medina and referred to them as evildoers and unbelievers. They had betrayed their own faith and the one true God by refusing to accept Muhammad's authority as the Prophet. Finally, in 627 Muhammad and the Muslims turned on Medina's last Jewish tribe. The men were executed, most of the women and children were sold into slavery, and homes and possessions were all confiscated. It was a unique event in Muhammad's life. It suggests uncharacteristic cruelty in a man who argued for peace and tolerance. Historians and theologians have tried to explain or rationalize the massacre for centuries, but with little agreement or understanding. Some say it just could not have happened or that Muhammad's followers did it.

Most historians say, however, that it appears that Muhammad at least condoned the killings, whether he did or did not order them himself.

Muhammad's ruthless demonstrations of power and strength are reported by Ibn Ishaq but have been denied as untruths by other Islamic historians. Whatever the truth, Muhammad fought enemies and proved his determination, but he also struggled to build alliances. He took multiple wives—nine altogether. The first ones were daughters of his close friends and advisors, Abu Bakr and an early convert named Omar. Abu Bakr's daughter Aisha was reported to be Muhammad's favorite. He married one woman who had been captured during a battle, thus sealing a pact of peace with her tribe. Muhammad gave his youngest daughter, Fatima, in marriage to Ali, his adopted son and cousin. And after the massacre of the Jewish tribe, Muhammad married one woman captive, Rayhana, who had ties to two of the three Jewish tribes.

Conquering Mecca and Arabia

Perhaps all the alliance building through marriages helped Muhammad to use more peaceful and compassionate means to triumph over his enemies in Mecca. Determined to liberate the Kaaba from pagan hands, Muhammad led a conquering army to Mecca in 630. Along the way, as they marched through the desert, almost every tribe they met joined them, until they were ten thousand strong. The Meccan defenders outside the city gave way without a struggle, and Muhammad took Mecca with no use of force at all. Many in the city, especially the ruling elite, feared vengeance, but Muhammad had come in peace. He ordered all the idols in the Kaaba destroyed and dedicated the temple to Allah. He declared, "Truth hath come; darkness hath vanished away."[27] Muhammad announced that his enemies were forgiven and that his return to Mecca was not conquest but liberation. Many people in Mecca converted to Islam, and the Quraysh swore allegiance to him.

All over Arabia, people heard of Muhammad's ascendancy and the greatness of Islam. Clans and tribes offered their submission to Muhammad and became united under his rule. At the age of sixty, Muhammad had triumphed. He was the all-powerful leader of Arabia, but he did not stay in Mecca to rule. Instead, he appointed a governor of Mecca and returned to Medina to live out his life. He continued to live simply in the compound at the mosque and use the revelations and visions that still came to him for the benefit of his people.

The Religion of Islam

It was in Medina that Muhammad revealed and gave final form to the five pillars of the Islamic faith. The first pillar is the profession of faith. It is the creed of every Muslim: "There is no God but God and Muhammad is the Messenger of God."[28] The second pillar is prayer and requires

Devout Muslims make a once-in-a-lifetime pilgrimage to Mecca. The pilgrimage represents the unity of all Muslims and their oneness under God. It is also a remembrance of Muhammad's final pilgrimage to Mecca.

five daily prayers through which each Muslim has a direct relationship with God. The third pillar is almsgiving. This means that Muslims recognize that social responsibility is a part of their service to God and that they give a set portion of their income to the poor. The fourth pillar of faith is fasting. Every year, during the month of Ramadan—when Muhammad received the first revelation—Muslims fast from dawn until sunset to help themselves develop a better relationship with God and remind themselves of the sufferings of the poor. The fifth pillar is the duty to make a once-in-a-lifetime pilgrimage to Mecca—the hajj. The pilgrimage represents the unity of all Muslims and of the worldwide community and its oneness under God. It is also a remembrance of Muhammad's own last pilgrimage to Mecca.

After he conquered Mecca and returned to Medina, Muhammad made one final pilgrimage to Mecca in 632. He prayed at the Kaaba, now sacred and dedicated to Allah alone. During his five-day visit, he spoke several times to the gathered people for what would be the last time. He preached, for example, that there was to be no revenge for anything that had happened before Islam ruled Arabia. He said that no one was to be forced to convert to Islam and that Christians and Jews had to be respected. He explained that the Quran that had been preached to them over the years contained all anyone needed to know to be one with God. He said, "Ponder my words. I have left with you knowledge which, if you follow it, will preserve you for ever from going astray; the words of Allah and the injunctions of His apostle. Know that every Muslim is brother to every Muslim. No man may take anything from his brother save what is freely given."[29]

Muhammad's Death

Only a few weeks after returning to Medina from his final pilgrimage, Muhammad fell ill with what is today believed to have been bacterial meningitis. After several days of worsening sickness, he died in Aisha's room, and she said that she was holding him in her arms as he drew his last breath. It was June 8, 632, and Muhammad was sixty-three years old. Aisha's father, Abu Bakr, broke the news to the waiting people who filled the compound. He said, "O people! Lo! As for him who used to worship Muhammad, Muhammad is dead. But as for him who used to worship God, God is alive and dies not." Then, as words of comfort to the frightened and grieving people, Abu Bakr recited a verse of the Quran: "And Muhammad is but a messenger; messengers the like of whom have passed away before him. Will it be that, when he dies or is slain, you will turn back on your heels? He who turneth back doth no hurt to God, and God will reward the thankful."[30]

The Prophet Muhammad was dead, but God was alive, Islam was alive, and now it would be up to Muhammad's followers and successors to believe and to spread the word of God.

Chapter 4

The Expansion of Islam

Muhammad had been a religious leader, a political leader, and a military leader. It seemed impossible that any one person could take his place. The loss of Muhammad, however, did not stop the growth of Islam nor stem the energy and enthusiasm of his followers. The Muslims worked devoutly to maintain and expand the sacred community of Islam. They had a holy book of their own, the Quran, as their foundation. With the religious guidance of the Quran, political and military leadership fell to the first four so-called patriarchal caliphs, who had been relatives and close followers of Muhammad himself. Within the first hundred years after Muhammad's death, the religion exploded throughout Eurasia in ever-widening circles.

The Holy Book for Guidance

By the time Muhammad died, all the suras had been written down, at Muhammad's direction, by some of the few literate scribes in Medina and Mecca who were his followers. Muhammad always memorized all the verses he was given and then recited them to his followers and to the scribes who recorded the words. In the beginning, says Islamic scholar Mohammad Shafi, "The scribes would write on what ever material was available at the moment. Thus the writing medium ranged from a stone, the leaf of a palm tree, shoulder-bone of a camel, the membrane on the inside of a deer-skin, a parchment or a papyrus. These writings were stored in a corner of the Prophet's room and later, perhaps, in a separate room or office near the Prophet's room."[31]

In Medina one of the early scribes was a teenager named Zayd ibn Thabit. Zayd was eager to learn and record the verses Muhammad recited, and eventually Muhammad put him in charge of keeping the written records and organizing them appropriately. Other followers were official memorizers, who practiced carefully memorizing and repeating the exact words of Muhammad's revelations. After Muhammad's death, some of the memorizers helped Zayd compile all the verses into a book. The resulting first handwritten copy of the Quran was kept and guarded by one of Muhammad's wives. About fifteen years later, Zayd and his group handwrote several more copies for the use of Muslims who lived far from Medina so that the verses they had available would be absolutely accurate.

Choosing a Successor

Even with the carefully preserved book of the Quran, however, determining who would assume the role of the leader of Islam after Muhammad was not easy. No one else was a prophet or able to receive revelations from God, and Muhammad had named no successor before his death. He had no surviving sons who could take on the role of leader, as was the usual custom in Arabia. None of Muhammad's nine wives after Khadija had any children. Of Khadija's four daughters, two preceded Muhammad in death, as did the adopted freed slave Zayd. Only Muhammad's daughter Fatima lived close to her father, but she died just a few months after Muhammad. Fatima and her husband Ali had two sons—direct descendants of Muhammad, but they were young. Ali, however, as Muhammad's blood relation and the first child to accept Islam, was a close, trusted confidant of Muhammad. Muhammad's longtime friend Abu Bakr, the father of Muhammad's favorite wife, Aisha, was a close ally too and related through marriage. It was logical to the loyal members of Muhammad's inner circle that one of these two men should take over the leadership, but the group disagreed as to the ultimate choice.

One faction of the believers closest to Muhammad thought Ali should be the successor; Ali was cousin, adopted son, and son-in-law through

After Muhammad's death, the first four caliphs (pictured) who led Islam had direct ties to the Prophet. Under the first of these caliphs, Abu Bakr, Islam began to expand beyond Arabia.

his marriage to Fatima. Others chose Abu Bakr instead, as father-in-law and best friend and supporter from the very beginning. In addition, Muhammad had given Abu Bakr the title "The Most Truthful," and when Muhammad had lain ill, he appointed Abu Bakr to be the imam, the leader of the daily prayers at the compound. Ultimately, the assembly of Muhammad's companions chose Abu Bakr as Islam's first caliph. (*Caliph* means "successor.") Despite his disappointment and some initial objections, Ali, as well as all of Muhammad's other close confidants, eventually pledged loyalty to the new caliph. Abu Bakr would be the first of the four patriarchal caliphs—leaders of Islam with direct ties to Muhammad himself. Abu Bakr was caliph from 632 until he died in 634. His most important contribution was to maintain the union of Arabia under Muslim rule and to begin its expansion outside of Arabia.

Could Islam Survive?

As soon as the news of Muhammad's death spread, many of the Bedouin tribes revolted, refusing to recognize Abu Bakr's legitimacy and rejecting Islam. Islamic historian Fazl Ahmad explains, "The death of the holy Prophet led some people to think that Islam was going to end with him. Many tribes had entered the fold of Islam only a short time before. They were by no means firm in the new faith. Many of them, now, showed signs of bolting out of the fold of Islam."[32] The alliances that Muhammad had worked so hard to forge were falling apart. Abu Bakr launched a military campaign against these rebelling tribes, and by 633 he had successfully brought them back under Muslim control.

With all of the Arabian Peninsula again united under Islam, Abu Bakr turned his attention to the larger world. He was a military man, and he believed that only by expanding Arabia's influence would Islam be secure from outside threats. He was also a fervent Muslim who wanted to bring the world to God. Abu Bakr declared jihad, or holy war, against the Byzantine Empire, which he saw as an enemy of Islam. The Quran said that such a war was justified when Islam was threatened. His first military expedition, however, was against the Persian Empire, in the portion that is now Iraq. The Sassanids were unbelievers who had

Rules of War

Muslim wars of conquest were fought for the most part under the religious principles established by the Quran and by the sayings of Muhammad. Muhammad had lain down many rules about how to conduct war, from requiring kind treatment for prisoners of war to forbidding mutilating an enemy's face. He believed that Muslim armies should behave morally, and his precepts about military behavior led to conduct quite different from that which was usual for conquering armies. One of his sayings about war is, "When Muslims enter enemy territory, they should not strike terror into the general population. They should permit no ill-treatment of common folk."

When Abu Bakr took over as first caliph, he added to Muhammad's proscriptions. One of his rules for his conquering armies was, "Public buildings and fruit-bearing trees (and food crops) are not to be damaged." Islam did not conquer through destruction or by causing misery and starvation for conquered peoples. In large part the empire and its religion succeeded so well because they conquered so gently.

Quoted in Mirza Bashiruddin Mahmud Ahmad, *Life of Muhammad*. Tilford, Surry, UK: Raqeem/Islam International, 1990.

vowed to crush Islam. The initial attack was successful, but before Abu Bakr could strike in the heart of the empire, he became ill with a severe fever. He knew he was dying and remembered the disagreements after Muhammad's death. Wanting to avoid a repeat of dissension at his own death, Abu Bakr named a successor. The second caliph would be Omar, another of Muhammad's fathers-in-law and an early convert to Islam. Omar was a capable military man and a powerful politician who would be able to keep the Islamic world united.

Omar's Caliphate

Omar was Islam's leader from 634 to 644 CE. Omar continued Abu Bakr's campaign to expand Islam's influence, and he was swiftly and remarkably successful. He called himself "Commander of the Faithful,"[33] as well as caliph, and the faithful joined his armies and fought willingly under his orders. Omar struck at the Persian Empire along its borders, and also at the Byzantine Empire in Syria and Egypt. His campaigns were wars of conquest, and one by one areas fell into Muslim hands. By 640 all of Mesopotamia and most of Syria and Palestine were under Omar's control. He conquered Egypt in 642, and by 643 the Persian Empire had collapsed and was in Muslim hands, except for the easternmost parts.

The speed at which Arabia overwhelmed the territories surrounding them can be hard to understand. Historians Judith M. Bennett and C. Warren Hollister explain:

> Their spectacular conquests resulted in part from the youthful vigor of Islam and in part from the weakness of its enemies. When Arab armies appeared on their borders, the Persian and Byzantine Empires had just concluded a long, desperate conflict that left both powers exhausted. Furthermore, the Byzantine government had so mistreated the Monophysite Christians [a dissenting sect of Christianity] of Syria and Egypt that they seem to have welcomed new, more tolerant governors.[34]

Islam's method of governing was part of its genius and a large part of the reason for its continued success. Omar built a political system that did not oppress the conquered people. Nor did he try to control all the conquered territory from a centralized government, as did the Persians and Byzantines. Initially, says Hollister, the Arabs came "afire with religious zeal, lured by the wealth and luxuries of the civilized world."[35] Coming as they did from a poor and desolate land, they were in awe of the great cities and the richness of the goods owned by the rulers. They plundered and claimed the bounty as they had done when they raided Arabian caravans. This was part of their cultural tradition. Arabia became wealthy on its conquests, but it ruled without cruelty and did not place insupportable burdens on the populace. Omar allowed the conquered lands to keep their own religions, languages, and customs. He even left their governments largely in place. All he imposed was an Islamic governor, or amir, who reported to the caliph, and a financial officer to oversee the collection of taxes. Amirs and financial officers were forbidden to use their power to get rich at the expense of the people they oversaw.

One example of the tolerance with which Omar treated defeated people is the pact that he signed with the Christians of Jerusalem when it surrendered to his armies. The pact reads, in part:

> This is the safety given by a servant of God, the leader of the faithful, Omar ibn al Khattab. . . . This safety is for their life, property, church and cross, for the healthy and the sick and for all their co-religionists. Their churches shall neither be used as residence nor shall they be demolished. No harm shall be done to their churches or their boundaries. There shall be no decrease in their crosses or riches. There shall neither be any compulsion in religion nor shall they be harmed.[36]

Tradition says that while Omar was in Jerusalem to sign the peace treaty, he went to visit the largest Christian church in the city. While he was there, the time for Muslim prayer came, and the bishop of the church told him to go ahead and pray in the church. Omar refused, saying, "No, if I do so, the Muslims may one day make this an excuse for taking over the church from you."[37] Instead, Omar went outside and said his prayers on the church steps. Afterward, he gave the bishop a letter directing that Muslims could not use even the steps for religious purposes.

The Jews and Christians in the conquered Byzantine territories were treated as well as the people of Jerusalem. They were grateful and happy for the religious tolerance, since they had been persecuted under the Byzantines. Omar instituted two tiers of taxes for these peoples that were tolerable, too. One tax was on landowners with agricultural wealth; the other was on non-Muslims for practicing their own religions. The

The split between Shia and Sunni sects of Islam was the first major division in the Muslim world, but it was not the last. Islam has many sects today. Sufism, for example, is a mystical religious movement that arose during the Umayyad dynasty and by the tenth century became a powerful force in Islam. Sufis reject worldliness and concentrate on meditation and self-denial in order to develop a personal relationship with God. The movement emphasizes God's love for humanity instead of the Sunni emphasis on God's authority. Sufism defines holy war as the struggle within each human as he or she strives to overcome sin and distance from God. Sufis attempt to live in strict obedience to the Quran and Islamic laws. Sufism is not so much a completely separate sect as it is a religious order of missionaries within Islam.

Centuries after Sufism arose, an Indian Muslim named Mirza Ghulam Ahmad began a Muslim sect called Ahmadiyya Islam. This sect believes that Ahmad is a prophet, like Muhammad. Ahmadiyyas are reformers who believe in nonviolence and claim that holy war means only a peaceful battle with nonbelievers. Most Muslims see Ahmad's claim to prophecy and his reinterpretation of the Quran as heresy. Several other smaller Islamic sects exist today, such the Wahhabi (in Saudi Arabia), the Khariji (the sect that assassinated Ali), and the Alawi (mostly in Syria). In the modern world about 84 percent of Muslims are Sunni, some 10 percent Shia, and the rest follow the smaller sects.

taxes were not an extreme hardship, but they did encourage nonbelievers to listen to the Muslims preaching the religion of Islam. Although not forced to do so, many people converted willingly to Islam. They were attracted by the messages of God's love, and equality, tolerance, and justice for everyone—and of course, they no longer paid the religion tax, either. Omar's Arabian nation may have conquered through military force, but it won the loyalty of the peoples by ruling justly and kindly. In Egypt the policy of tolerance and nonrepressive political control was continued, and Egypt soon accepted Islam. The Persian Empire gradually converted to Islam as well, although the Persians kept many traditions and parts of their own culture and Zoroastrian religion.

Omar, says historian Nazeer Ahmed, "laid the foundation of Islamic civilization."[38] By the end of Omar's ten-year rule, Medina was the capital city of a true Islamic Empire. It was the largest empire in the world at that time. In addition to building an empire, Omar also developed the first Islamic calendar and established the *diwan*. The *diwan* was a governmental council that controlled the empire's finances and distributed the wealth acquired from conquered lands to all Arabs and the Muslim soldiers in what was supposed to be a fair and equitable way. It was a kind of pension system or welfare state for the Muslim people.

Cracks in Islamic Unity: The Third Caliph

Omar was assassinated by a disgruntled Persian Christian in 644, but before he died, he chose a committee of six men who were to decide on the next caliph. The committee narrowed their choice to two men—Ali (who was, of course, of the Hashim clan of Muhammad) and a member of the Umayyad clan named Uthman. They eventually chose Uthman, even though he had initially been fiercely opposed to Muhammad. Abu Bakr and his daughter Aisha were of the Umayyad clan too, but they had supported Muhammad from the beginning. Uthman was a longtime, loyal convert to Islam, but he was not one of the original followers of Muhammad. He was, however, a skillful politician and military leader. The committee thought that he was a more practical choice for caliph than Ali, who was seen as more religious and philosophical. Ali had become dissatisfied with the direction Islam was taking. He believed that it was straying from the religious and ethical teachings of Muhammad's revelations. Uthman became the third caliph because the new empire, the committee thought,

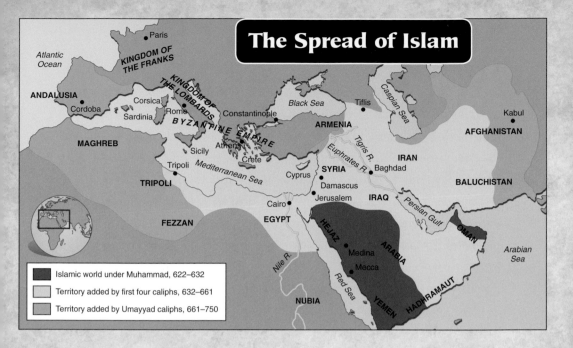

The Spread of Islam

Atlantic Ocean

Paris

KINGDOM OF THE FRANKS

KINGDOM OF THE LOMBARDS

ANDALUSIA

Cordoba

Corsica

Rome

Sardinia

BYZANTINE EMPIRE

Constantinople

Black Sea

Tiflis

ARMENIA

Caspian Sea

Kabul

AFGHANISTAN

MAGHREB

Sicily

Athens

Crete

Tripoli

Mediterranean Sea

Cyprus

Euphrates R.

Tigris R.

SYRIA

Baghdad

IRAN

BALUCHISTAN

TRIPOLI

Damascus

Jerusalem

IRAQ

Persian Gulf

OMAN

Cairo

EGYPT

FEZZAN

HEJAZ

Medina

Mecca

ARABIA

Arabian Sea

Nile R.

Red Sea

NUBIA

YEMEN

HADHRAMAUT

- Islamic world under Muhammad, 622–632
- Territory added by first four caliphs, 632–661
- Territory added by Umayyad caliphs, 661–750

needed a practical, not-so-religious man to help it grow and stabilize.

Uthman ruled as caliph from 644 to 656 CE, and during his twelve years as caliph he conquered the remaining Persian territories, took Cyprus from the Byzantine Empire, and conquered Libya. Under his direction, a definitive text of the Quran was compiled in written form, although some Muslims questioned whether Uthman's Quran was error free. But Uthman was not popular among the Islamic people, and his choice caused the first major rift in the Islamic world. One faction of Muslims approved of Uthman as caliph; the other believed that only Ali, as the adopted son, son-in-law, and cousin of Muhammad, was the rightful caliph. Ali's supporters thought that the leader of Islam should be a direct descendant of Muhammad and had been angry and disappointed when Ali was passed over for caliph. Supporters of the Umayyad clan, on the other hand, rejected bloodline as a qualification and insisted that Uthman was the legitimate head of the empire because he was supported by the most powerful Quraysh leaders. Aisha was a firm supporter of the Umayyads, too. Old clan rivalries and loyalties grew large in importance. Uthman appointed members of his clan to important government positions, and this favoritism angered other clans. He spent money lavishly and seriously mishandled government finances.

Civil War

In 655 civil war broke out in the Muslim world. In 656, during a furious riot in Medina—from which Uthman ruled—rioters broke into
Uthman's house and killed him as he sat reading the Quran. It was
the first time that an Islamic leader was killed by fellow Muslims. The
Islamic leaders of Medina chose Ali as the fourth and last of the patriarchal caliphs, but his rule did not last long and was marked by continued strife. After Ali's selection the Umayyads, who were everywhere in
powerful government positions, rose against him and declared a caliph
of their own in 658. He was Mu'awiyya, the governor of Damascus in
Syria. Despite efforts at reconciliation, neither side would give up.

The violence of the civil war continued until Ali had to flee Medina
for the town of Kufa in Iraq. From there he attempted to fight the
Umayyads and then had to fight a group of dissenting rebels from his
own army. In 661 Ali was assassinated by a soldier of his own faction.
By that time the powerful Umayyad armies had already defeated Ali's
army and were in control of the Islamic Empire. Mu'awiyya moved the
capital from Medina to Damascus, which would remain the capital of
the Islamic Empire for one hundred years.

The Umayyad Dynasty

The era of the patriarchal caliphate was at an end, and the Umayyad
dynasty had begun. It lasted from 661 to 750 CE and was a time of
dramatic Islamic expansion and conquest. The dynasty represented the
majority of Muslims, but never again were all Muslims united under
one belief system. The faction that had supported Ali continued to be
dissatisfied with the seemingly secular and, to them, illegitimate rule of
the Umayyads. This split between Ali's supporters and the Umayyads
eventually led to two different forms of Islam. Even though Ali's faction
recognized the authority of the caliphs in practice, they appointed their
own religious leaders, imams, who were the ultimate authorities on the
word of God. Ali's supporters never accepted the religious authority of
the Umayyad caliphs. Bennett and Hollister explain:

In time, this movement evolved into a distinct form of Islam, known as Shi'ism, which held that the true caliphs—the descendants of Muhammad through Fatima and Ali—were sinless, infallible, and possessed of a body of secret knowledge hidden in the Quran. In these beliefs, Shi'i Muslims were distinct from the majority of Muslims, the Sunnis, who based their faith firmly on the Quran and the practices of the prophet.[39]

The Umayyad dynasty, begun with Mu'awiyya, was more interested in empire than religious authenticity. It expanded Islamic conquests in North Africa, attacked the Byzantine capital of Constantinople, and claimed for Islam the region of Iberia, which included most of Spain, Portugal, and Andorra. For a time, it even ruled southern France. The attack on Constantinople eventually failed, however, and Islamic armies were never able to push into most of Europe or conquer the center of the Byzantine Empire, but the Islamic Empire was larger and more powerful than the Byzantine Empire ever was. Bennett and Hollister say, "By 750, Muslims held more than half of the territory once governed by Rome."[40]

Like the rulers before them, the Umayyads did not attempt to force religious conversion on non-Muslims. As long as these people accepted Muslim rule, paid their taxes, and did not try to convert Muslims, they lived in an atmosphere of tolerance and acceptance, but the religion of Islam was so compelling that many conquered peoples did convert. Nevertheless, the Umayyad rulers were never as interested in spreading Islam as Muhammad's followers had been. They were concerned with expansion and empire. The patriarchal caliphs had believed in the principles of equality and simple living. The Umayyad rulers acted and lived like kings. The Jewish Virtual Library says:

They separated their court from the Muslim community and surrounded themselves with wealth and ceremony. This was a model of leadership based on the idea that authority was vested in super-normal individuals, a radically different turn of events in the Muslim world. . . . Under the Umayyads, then, the caliphate became something much closer to a monarchy rather than a tribal or religious leadership.[41]

Beginning with Mu'awiyya, the Umayyads behaved like royalty in another way. They turned the caliphate into a hereditary dynasty, with son succeeding father as caliph. This sometimes meant that the empire was ruled by cruel or weak caliphs. Many Muslims were fiercely opposed to the Umayyads because they seemed to ignore the fundamental principles of leadership laid down by Muhammad. Even today, modern Muslim historians refer to the Umayyad period as a "kingdom," not a "caliphate." Despite their flaws, however, the Umayyads maintained control of a large and far-flung empire through their domination as powerful monarchs. By the end of the Umayyad dynasty, Islam and the Arabs were a world force and poised to become the most advanced civilization in Eurasia.

Chapter 5

What Is the Legacy of the Rise of Islam?

By 750 the once backward and insignificant Arabs had crafted a true empire that achieved equilibrium with the Byzantine Empire and Western Christendom. Judith M. Bennett and C. Warren Hollister say, "Historians sometimes talk of these three civilizations as the 'three heirs' of Rome or even as the 'three siblings.'"[42] They could not conquer each other militarily. Instead, each spread its sphere of influence in different directions. However, while Christendom (western Europe) was still mired in primitive ignorance and the Byzantine Empire was an exhausted, worn-out civilization trying to maintain the status quo, the Islamic Empire was a vibrant, energetic, eager culture. According to Bennett and Hollister, the Islamic Empire "was by far the greatest of the three civilizations that encircled the Mediterranean Sea."[43] By the time the Umayyad dynasty came to an end, little more than one hundred years after Muhammad's death, Islam entered its golden age.

The Abbasids

In 750 the Abbasids overthrew the Umayyad dynasty. Claiming the right to the caliphate because of their descent from one of Muhammad's uncles, they were supported in their rise by the Shiites, even though the Abbasids were Sunnis. The Abbasids continued the expansion of the empire by turning to the east, to Asia, instead of vying for power with the Byzantines and western Europe. They successfully fought the Chinese in Central Asia, taking over all the territory from Morocco and into China, and then conquered much of India and Indonesia. Although they abandoned the attempt to conquer the Byzantines, the empire was so weakened that it was forced to pay a heavy yearly tribute to the Islamic Empire to avoid military attacks. In 762, the Abbasids moved the capital of the empire to Baghdad, which became a great world city and the center of a forward-thinking and flourishing culture. The US Department of Defense's Cultural Resources Program says:

> The Abbasid period (750–1258) is considered the golden age of Muslim rule, a brilliant and tolerant civilization that encouraged scientific learning and the translation and updating of classics from other cultures. . . . By the year 900, the population of Baghdad was 1.5 million, larger than any European city and surpassed only by the great Chinese urban centers Beijing and Shanghai.[44]

Politically, the Abbasid dynasty was both tolerant and innovative. Instead of maintaining all power in the hands of the Arab elite, it employed the skills of people from many lands and cultures. United by the Arab language, Persians, Syrians, Christians, Jews, and many other peoples participated in the government and its bureaucracy with real decision-making power. The Arabs drew knowledge and methods of governmental administration from the Persian and Byzantine Empires. The financial system, banking system, and gathering of taxation across the empire were maintained by the administrative skill of multinational peoples. The Abbasid caliphs prized merit and capability. Even lowborn individuals without elite or aristocratic ties could rise high in the power structure if they had ability and useful knowledge.

Life in the Abbasid Dynasty

Under the Abbasids the Islamic Empire eagerly absorbed useful customs, inventions, intellectual advances, and business practices from any civilization it came across. Most of these cultures enriched and

What Happened to the Golden Age?

The Islamic Empire was so vast that maintaining control everywhere gradually became impossible. Revolts in Persia and North Africa weakened the empire, as did independently ruled regions that pretended allegiance to the Abbasid caliphs but did not practice it. Eventually, the Abbasids became figureheads, with Shiite rulers governing Iran and Iraq until they were overthrown by Sunni Turks. When the non-Islamic Mongols invaded and sacked Baghdad in 1258, it marked the end of Islam's golden age.

Muslims were no longer united under one political system with unified interpretations of Islam. The empire splintered into isolated communities with their own belief systems. Tolerance died. Intellectual liberalism that encouraged skepticism led many educated Muslims to reject some orthodox Islamic laws. Other Muslims, followers of splinter groups, accused these fellow Muslims of heresy. They were considered nonbelievers. To some Muslim sects, any nonbelievers became infidels who should be aggressively attacked in defense of Islam; to their way of thinking, the Quran allowed jihad against them.

Different sects argued about how to follow the Quran's precepts. As time passed, Sunni and Shia fought each other for power and religious rightness. The European colonialism of the nineteenth century turned some Muslims further toward militant Islam. Jihad for them was authorized by the Quran against all non-Muslims because holy war is always justifiable when Islam is threatened or denied. Many historians argue that modern radical Islam has its origins in the end of the golden age and the events that followed its collapse.

benefited the Arab civilization, but—as in all medieval civilizations of the time—many classes of people were left out. The peasants and unskilled laborers gained little and continued to struggle in poverty. Slavery remained an accepted practice, and the empire imported vast numbers of slaves from Africa and elsewhere. Women saw their status reduced. Hollister explains:

> The teachings of the Koran [Quran] had tended to raise the status of Arab women above the level of pre-Islamic Arabia, with its male-dominated tribal culture and its unrestrained polygamy (Muhammad limited his male followers to four wives only). But the Abbasid era witnessed the spread of severely anti-feminist customs, partly Persian in inspiration: the seclusion of women in private quarters such as harems; the hiding of women's faces and bodies behind veils and draperies. For all the brilliance of Abbasid civilization, women were distinctly better off in the monogamous environments of Byzantium and Western Christendom.[45]

For male citizens of the Islamic Empire, especially in the rich, powerful cities such as Baghdad, life could be both luxurious and exciting. Religious tolerance continued to be the rule, and while still taxed for their religion, Christians and Jews, along with Muslims, often reaped the rewards of being part of the superpower that was the Islamic Empire. Trade was extensive throughout the vast empire and beyond. Baghdad, for instance, imported silks and spices from India and China. It acquired gold and ivory from Africa and honey and furs from Scandinavia. Grains, metals, and woods came from all over the East and from Europe.

Commercial goods provided luxury and leisure for Baghdad, but the trade in ideas and inventions was perhaps more important. From China came the knowledge of how to make paper. From India came the so-called Arabic numerals and the mathematical concept of zero. From within Persia came the architectural skills that enabled the Abbasids of Baghdad to build a glittering, awe-inspiring city with water fountains, public baths, minarets, mosques, and an imperial palace that covered one-third of a circular city 12 miles (19.3 km) in diameter.

The teachings of the Quran raised the status of women, but women experienced many changes under the Abbasid dynasty. Among these changes was the requirement that women hide their faces and bodies beneath veils.

Seeking Wisdom

As the empire's wealth grew and contact with other cultures exploded, intellectual life flourished. Muhammad had once said that "the ink of scholars is more precious than the blood of martyrs."[46] Muslims avidly embraced education and learning as an important part of their faith, and this intellectual enthusiasm transformed the Arab world and produced a lasting legacy. Hollister says:

> The untutored Arab from the desert became the cultural heir of Greece, Rome, Persia, and India, and within less than two centuries of the Prophet's death, Islamic culture had reached the level of a mature, sophisticated civilization. Its mercurial rise was a consequence of the Arabs' success in absorbing the great civilized traditions of their conquered peoples and employing these traditions in a cultural synthesis both new and unique. Islam borrowed, but never without digesting. What it drew from other civilizations it transmuted and made its own.[47]

The caliph Harun al-Rashid, who ruled from 786 to 809, established a library and scientific academy in Baghdad. In this huge complex he stored all the books and manuscripts that his grandfather, his father, and he had collected from all parts of the empire. Al-Rashid's son, Caliph al-Ma'moun, expanded the academy and organized it so that one wing of the complex was dedicated to each subject. People named it the House of Wisdom. Scholars and educated men of every faith and from every corner of the empire gathered at the House of Wisdom and worked under the patronage of the caliphs. Historian Subhi al-Azzawi explains, "In this Academy, translators, scientists, scribes, authors, men of letters, writers . . . copyists and others used to meet every day for translation, reading, writing, scribing, discourse, dialogue and discussion. Many manuscripts and books in various scientific subjects and philosophical concepts and ideas, and in different languages were translated there."[48] Wisdom and education were so valued during the Abbasids' reign that sometimes books and ancient manuscripts were claimed as war booty instead of more traditional goods. Once, after a military struggle with the Byzantines, the treaty required a copy of a book written by the Greek astronomer Ptolemy be turned over to the Abbasids as a condition of peace.

The languages used in the House of Wisdom included Arabic (into which books were translated), Farsi, Hebrew, Aramaic, Syriac, Greek,

Latin, and Sanskrit. Some of the great works translated there included those of the famous Greek physician Hippocrates; the philosophers Aristotle and Plato; the scientists and mathematicians Archimedes, Pythagoras, and Euclid, and the Indian astronomer Brahmagupta. The scholars of the House of Wisdom found their work made much easier with the introduction of papermaking from China. Baghdad had paper mills, and by the end of the Abbasid era it boasted thirty-six different libraries and one hundred bookshops and publishers.

Golden Discoveries

As time passed and knowledge was absorbed, the scholars at the House of Wisdom became researchers, inventors, and discoverers. They had learned from Aristotle, and agreed with him, that mathematics was the foundation of all science. But Roman numerals did not lend themselves well to calculations. Even multiplication and division were cumbersome processes when calculated with Roman letters used to represent numbers. When knowledge of Hindu numbers reached Baghdad, the greatest Islamic mathematician of the ninth century, Muhammad ibn Musa al-Khwarizmi, immediately understood their value. Mathematical calculations were easy to perform and check for accuracy. Al-Khwarizmi wrote a famous book, *On the Calculation with Hindu Numerals*, which revolutionized mathematics in the empire and in the West. The new "Arabic" numerals spread quickly around the world. Al-Khwarizmi invented algebra, developed the use of the symbol x for unknown quantities, and demonstrated a method of resolving quadratic equations.

Caliph al-Ma'moun built an observatory for the scholars of astronomy at the House of Wisdom. It was placed on the outskirts of Baghdad and used by the astronomers to add their own commentaries and discoveries to the observations in the ancient texts that had been translated. Although they did not have telescopes—the invention of which lay far in the future—the astronomers did have the astrolabe. An ancient Greek invention, the astrolabe is an instrument that is basically a brass protractor with a sighting rod attached. Using an astrolabe, the observer can measure the altitude of the sun, planets, and stars;

In a later era, astronomers and other scholars explore new areas of learning. Scientific endeavor and education were valued throughout the Islamic Empire.

discover the time of sunset or sunrise on any given date; and perform many other astronomical computations. The instrument allows astronomers to determine how the sky looks from a specific place at a particular time. Historian David A. King says that Abbasid astronomers improved on and perfected the ancient concept of the astrolabe until it was "a veritable scientific work of art."[49]

One of the most famous Islamic astronomers was al-Battani, who lived from 858 to 929 CE. He mapped the motion of the planets, developed a star map of the heavens, and corrected many errors in the mathematical observations of rotation and motion first described by Ptolemy in ancient Greece. Later the Islamic astronomer Abd-al-Rahman Al-Sufi, who lived from 903 to 986, correctly described the magnitude, or brightness, of the observable stars and became the first to discover galaxies, which he called "clouds." In about 964 he published a famous text called *Book of the Fixed Stars* and identified about one hundred new stars. Many of the names that the Arabs used for the stars are today used throughout the world. For example, Rigel, Betelgeuse, Deneb, Vega, Altair, Fomalhaut, and Aldebaran are Arabic star names used in Al-Sufi's book, which was eventually translated into Latin for European scientists. The Arabic names were adopted in Europe, where Christian astronomers strove to learn astronomy from Muslim ones.

Islam and Medicine

The golden age of the Abbasids kept all kinds of science alive in the Arab world at a time when the rest of the Eurasian world seemed to have abandoned intellectual pursuits. Nowhere is this scientific dedication and advance more obvious than in the discipline of medicine. Muhammad had declared—not as a message from Allah but as his own advice—that using medicine was in accordance with God's wishes. He once said, "O Servant of God, use medicine, because God hath not created a pain without a remedy for it."[50] Muhammad believed that a treatment existed for every illness and that God would not have created any disease for which there was not a cure. He spoke against superstitions and magic cures such as amulets, charms, and sorcery, and he argued that people should seek help only from experienced and knowledgeable medical practitioners. He insisted that even terrible diseases like the plague, leprosy, or cholera epidemics were not punishments from God. He explained, "Disease is not the wrath of Allah, because Prophets also suffered great pains, much greater than ordinary people."[51] And he said that people who were victims of epidemics were martyrs, not sinners.

With Muhammad's words as their inspiration, Muslims sought to learn all they could about health and disease. They did not believe that any illness was incurable and thought that all people with sickness should be cared for and treated. Not only at the House of Wisdom, but all across the Muslim world, medical practitioners and physicians studied the translated works of the foremost Greek physicians Galen and Hippocrates. These Muslim scientists preserved and learned Greek medical theories, experimented and expanded on them, and developed new medical procedures and treatments.

Islam and Hospitals

Some of the first real hospitals in the world were established by Muslims. They were not just asylums to house the sick until they died but institutions staffed with doctors who offered treatment and hope of recovery. Muhammad himself established a small, mobile military hospital for his armies, and the first Muslim hospital was organized in Damascus under the Umayyad dynasty. When the Abbasids came to power, the first caliph invited a Persian physician to establish a hospital in Baghdad. Then in the ninth century a new Baghdad hospital, called Audidi, was built under the leadership of the great Muslim physician and scientist Abu Bakr Mohammad Ibn Zakariya al-Razi. Al-Razi searched for the healthiest place in the city to build a hospital by going to different areas, hanging raw meat, and watching how quickly it rotted. The area where the meat lasted the longest was where he built the hospital.

The finished Audidi facility had two dozen doctors, separate wards for people with different conditions—such as fevers, diseases of the eyes, diarrhea, and injuries from accidents—and a medical library.

Ibn al-Haytham (965–1040 CE) was a mathematician from Basra, Iraq. He was so confident that he could solve any problem mathematically that he claimed he could dam the Nile River to prevent its periodic destructive flooding. Al-Hakim, the ruler of Egypt, asked Ibn al-Haytham to come to Cairo and do it. Full of confidence, al-Haytham went, but once he actually saw the Nile, he realized that damming it was not technologically possible. Knowing that the ruthless ruler would execute him for failure, al-Haytham pretended to be insane. So al-Hakim had him placed under house arrest in Cairo. There al-Haytham had the peace and quiet to concentrate on his scientific research, just as he wanted, until al-Hakim's death ten years later.

Al-Haytham became the world's first scientist. He insisted that all facts had to be proved before accepted as true. He developed the scientific method of experimentation and argued that facts must be empirically demonstrated. He studied optics, the science of light. The ancient Greeks taught that people could see because "vision rays" came out of the eye and struck objects. Al-Haytham demonstrated that light enters the eye, is focused, and then projected to the back of the eye. Using a device similar to a pinhole camera and applying geometry to his observations, he explained the light refraction that makes the sky change color at sunset, and he calculated the depth of the earth's atmosphere. Al-Haytham's famous work, *The Book of Optics*, later guided Western scientists to invent such things as eyeglasses, telescopes, and cameras.

Sicker patients were kept separate from healthier ones, and good food and cleanliness were emphasized. Author Michael Hamilton Morgan says, "By the year 1000, five major hospitals will have been built in

Abbasid Baghdad. These hospitals will serve multiple purposes, not unlike modern hospitals containing surgery centers, outpatient clinics, psychiatric wards, convalescent centers, and even nursing homes. And quite often they are free to those in need."[52] During the Abbasid caliphate, about thirty-four hospitals were established throughout the Muslim world; all of them followed al-Razi's model and were as modern and medically advanced as the hospitals of Baghdad.

Muslim Medical Progress

Al-Razi, who lived from 865 to 925, was the leading scholar of the golden age of Islam, and in medicine his contributions were remarkable. During his working life the few educated physicians in Europe depended on the medical teachings of Galen almost with blind faith. They did not question, observe, or experiment. As Galen had taught, they believed, for example, that the body was composed of four vital humors—blood, black bile, yellow bile, and phlegm. Illness was caused by an imbalance in these humors and usually had to be corrected by drawing off the patient's blood, or bloodletting. Al-Razi began his medical career by studying Galen, but he was a scientist and experimenter who questioned Galen's assumptions. Al-Razi wrote a book called *Doubts About Galen*. Morgan reports, "In *Doubts about Galen*, al-Razi explicitly questions whether the theory of humors can explain why giving a patient a hot drink causes his body temperature to rise much higher than the liquid itself; al-Razi holds that such a reaction would imply that there are certain other regulatory processes at work in the body that the humors do not address."[53]

Al-Razi's careful clinical observations and his willingness to explore alternative explanations for illnesses led him to the development of practical diagnosis and treatment. He was the first physician, for example, to differentiate between measles and smallpox and assert that they were different illnesses that needed different treatments and had different outcomes. He explained that fever was the body's way of fighting illness, and he was the first person to describe and diagnose hay fever or allergies, which he noticed occurred in some people when roses were in bloom. He described how to correctly diagnose diseases such as diabetes, colic in infants, and kidney stones. He treated depression and pain with poppies (the source of opium) because of its euphoric and

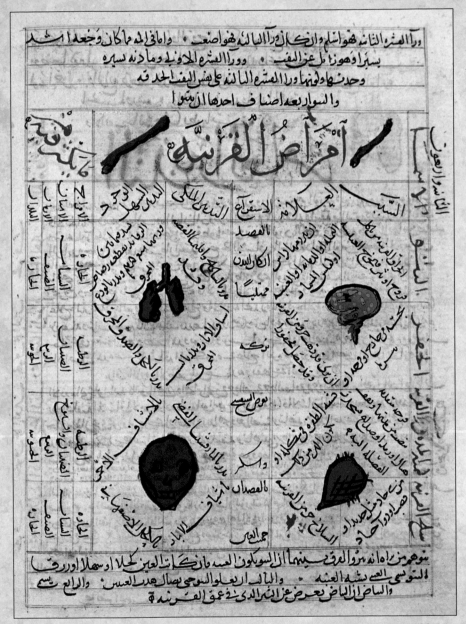

A page from Ibn Sina's Canon of Medicine *illustrates just a few of his observations and methods. The Persian physician's book was used in medical schools throughout the world for six hundred years.*

pain-numbing effects. He developed treatments for diseases by carefully experimenting on monkeys with various plant-based potions and with mercury in ointments. Mercury is an antiseptic and heals skin rashes, but it is also a poison. Eventually, al-Razi's experiments with mercury burned his eyes and caused blindness, but before that occurred, he had written more than two hundred books. One of them, *The Comprehensive Book of Medicine*, was a summary of all the medical knowledge he had acquired and became such an important medical manual that it was a standard medical text in Europe for hundreds of years.

Other great Islamic physicians followed al-Razi during the golden age—men who changed the course of medicine throughout the world. They include Al Zahrawi (later called Albucasis in Europe), who worked in Cordoba in Islamic Spain. Al Zahrawi lived from 936 to 1013 and was the father of modern surgery. He developed surgical procedures for treating bone fractures and performing mastectomies and dental surgeries, as well as using thread or wire to close torn or surgically severed arteries. Al Zahrawi also invented about two hundred surgical instruments such as forceps, surgical needles, syringes, and scalpels. The father of modern medicine is Abu Ali al-Husayn ibn Abd Allah ibn Sina (known as Avicenna in Europe). He was a Persian physician who lived from 980 to 1037. Ibn Sina was the first to explain how to use the experimental method in medicine and to use clinical trials to determine the efficacy of treatments. He outlined seven rules for experimenting with new drugs, including testing only one drug at a time, ensuring the drug's purity, and starting with as low a dose as possible in the first tests. He also recognized and explained contagious diseases and was the first to assert that tuberculosis is a contagious disease. Ibn Sina's book *Canon of Medicine* would be used in medical schools throughout the world for the next six hundred years.

Golden Literature

Literature, as well as scientific writing, thrived during the golden age. Muslim authors wrote beautiful poetry and short works of prose. The great poet Omar Khayyam, who lived from 1048 to 1131, wrote the

Rubaiyat, a book of poems in quatrains. A quatrain is a verse or poem of four lines, and *rubaiyat* means "quatrain" in Arabic. The *Rubaiyat* is considered a masterwork around the world. One famous quatrain is:

> A Book of Verses underneath the Bough,
> A Jug of Wine, a Loaf of Bread—and Thou
> Beside me singing in the Wilderness
> Oh, Wilderness were Paradise enow [enough]![54]

Perhaps the most famous work from the golden age is *One Thousand and One Nights*, a collection of stories from the Middle East and India. No one knows the author or the exact date it was published, except that it was sometime during the ninth century. It is the story of Scheherazade, the wife of an evil king who kills a new wife each day. Scheherazade saves herself and all other women who might fall victim to the king by telling him a new story each night he visits her and leaving each unfinished until the next night, for a thousand nights, until the king falls in love. From *One Thousand and One Nights* come the stories of Ali Baba, Sinbad the Sailor, and Aladdin.

The World's Indebtedness to Islam

All in all, says historian Zachariah Matthews, "The accomplishments of Islam's Golden Age are too numerous to mention."[55] From the Muslim world came developments as important as algebra and inventions as popular as toothbrushes, perfume, forged steel, soap, and fountain pens. For perhaps one thousand years, the Islamic civilization was the most advanced in the world. Without the Islamic Empire, it is likely that other world civilizations would not have seen their ancient knowledge preserved, nor perhaps would Western civilization have flourished in later times. The intellectual freedom, religious tolerance, and unifying atmosphere of the Islamic Empire truly changed the world.

Source Notes

Introduction: The Defining Characteristics of the Rise of Islam

1. Firas Alkhateeb, "What Was Special About Pre-Islamic Arabia?," Lost Islamic History. http://lostislamichistory.com.
2. Alkhateeb, "What Was Special About Pre-Islamic Arabia?"
3. C. Warren Hollister, *Medieval Europe: A Short History*, 5th ed. New York: Wiley, 1982, p. 70.
4. Royal Embassy of Saudi Arabia, "The Rise of Islam," 2013. www.saudiembassy.net.

Chapter One: What Conditions Led to the Rise of Islam?

5. Judith M. Bennett and C. Warren Hollister, *Medieval Europe: A Short History*, 10th ed. New York: McGraw-Hill, 2006, p. 69.
6. Alkhateeb, "What Was Special About Pre-Islamic Arabia?"
7. Lesley Hazleton, *The First Muslim: The Story of Muhammad*. New York: Riverhead, 2013, p. 110.
8. Hollister, *Medieval Europe*, p. 68.
9. Nihal Sahin Utku, "Arabia in the Pre-Islamic Period," Last Prophet .info, June 13, 2013. www.lastprophet.info.
10. Utku, "Arabia in the Pre-Islamic Period."

Chapter Two: Born into a Changing World

11. Hazleton, *The First Muslim*, p. 17.
12. Quoted in Hazleton, *The First Muslim*, p. 22.
13. Quoted in Hazleton, *The First Muslim*, p. 28.
14. Quoted in IslamicLandmarks, "Monastery of Bahira the Monk," 2013. www.islamiclandmarks.com.
15. Hazleton, *The First Muslim*, p. 61.
16. Mirza Bashiruddin Mahmud Ahmad, *Life of Muhammad*. Tilford, Surry, UK: Raqeem/Islam International, 1990.
17. Ibn Ishaq, *Sirat Rasoul Allah*, Internet Archive, p. 20. https://archive.org.

18. Quoted in Hazleton, *The First Muslim*, p. 78.
19. Quoted in Abraham Sarker, *Understand My Muslim People*. Newberg, OR: Barclay, 2004, p. 45.
20. Quoted in Mark A. Gabriel, *Jesus and Muhammad*. Lake Mary, FL: Charisma, 2004, p. 34.

Chapter Three: Muhammad's Faith
21. Quoted in Ibn Ishaq, *Sirat Rasoul Allah*, p. 21.
22. Ibn Ishaq, *Sirat Rasoul Allah*, p. 21.
23. Quoted in Hazleton, *The First Muslim*, pp. 96–97.
24. Religion of Islam, "Muhammad's Biography (Part 4 of 12): Persecution in Mecca," February 13, 2006. www.islamreligion.com.
25. Hazleton, *The First Muslim*, p. 107.
26. Quoted in Religion of Islam, "Muhammad's Biography (Part 5 of 12): Setting the Stage for Migration," February 13, 2006. www.islam religion.com.
27. Quoted in Religion of Islam, "Muhammad's Biography (Part 11 of 12): The Return to Mecca," February 13, 2006. www.islamreligion. com.
28. Quoted in Royal Embassy of Saudi Arabia, "The Five Pillars of Islam: About Saudi Arabia," 2013. www.saudiembassy.net.
29. Quoted in Ibn Ishaq, *Sirat Rasoul Allah*, p. 113.
30. Quoted in Religion of Islam, "Muhammad's Biography (Part 12 of 12): Bidding Farewell," February 13, 2006. www.islamreligion.com.

Chapter Four: The Expansion of Islam
31. Mohammad Shafi, "The Qur'an—How It Was Revealed and Compiled," Dar al Islam. www.daralislam.org.
32. Fazl Ahmad, "Hazrat Abu Bakr Siddiq: The First Caliph of Islam," Answering Christianity. www.answering-christianity.com.
33. Quoted in Aisha Stacey, "Omar, The Criterion (Part 3 of 3): The Commander of the Faithful," Religion of Islam, January 26, 2009. www.islamreligion.com.
34. Bennett and Hollister, *Medieval Europe*, pp. 85, 87.
35. Hollister, *Medieval Europe*, p. 70.
36. Quoted in Nazeer Ahmed, "Omar Ibn al Khattab," *History of Islam* (blog). http://historyofislam.com.
37. Quoted in *Islamic Bulletin*, "Omar bin Khattab (RA)—The Second Caliph of Islam." http://islamicbulletin.org.

38. Ahmed, "Omar Ibn al Khattab."

39. Bennett and Hollister, *Medieval Europe*, p. 88.

40. Bennett and Hollister, *Medieval Europe*, p. 88.

41. Jewish Virtual Library, "The Umayyad Caliphate," 2013. www.jew ishvirtuallibrary.org.

Chapter Five: What Is the Legacy of the Rise of Islam?

42. Bennett and Hollister, *Medieval Europe*, p. 68.

43. Bennett and Hollister, *Medieval Europe*, p. 68.

44. US Department of Defense, "The Rise of Islam (AD 633–)," Fort Drum Cultural Resources Program and the Center for Environmental Management of Military Lands: Colorado State University. www.cemml.colostate.edu.

45. Hollister, *Medieval Europe*, p. 75.

46. Quoted in Zachariah Matthews, "The Golden Age of Islam," Islamic Research Foundation International, October 2004. www.irfi.org.

47. Hollister, *Medieval Europe*, p. 77.

48. Subhi al-Azzawi, "The Abbasids' House of Wisdom in Baghdad," MuslimHeritage.com, February 7, 2007. www.muslimheritage.com.

49. David A. King, "Two Newly-Discovered Astrolabes from 'Abbasid Baghdad," *Suhayl: International Journal for the History of the Exact and Natural Sciences in Islamic Civilisation*, vol. 11, 2012, p. 103.

50. Quoted in M. Iqtedar Husain Farooqi, "Medicine of the Prophet (Tibb al-Nabvi)," Islamic Research Foundation International. www.irfi.org.

51. Quoted in Farooqi, "Medicine of the Prophet (Tibb al-Nabvi)."

52. Michael Hamilton Morgan, *Lost History: The Enduring Legacy of Muslim Scientists, Thinkers, and Artists*. Washington, DC: National Geographic Society, 2007, p. 212.

53. Morgan, *Lost History*, p. 187.

54. Omar Khayyam, *The Rubaiyat*, Internet Classics Archive. http://classics.mit.edu.

55. Matthews, "The Golden Age of Islam."

Important People During the Rise of Islam

Abbasids: The third of the Islamic caliphates to succeed Muhammad. The dynasty claimed descent from Muhammad's youngest uncle and ruled from 750 to 1258, during Islam's golden age.

Abu Bakr: The first caliph of the first Islamic caliphate, known as the patriarchal caliphate. He was Muhammad's longtime friend and supporter and, through his daughter Aisha, Muhammad's father-in-law. Abu Bakr held Islamic Arabia together after Muhammad's death and began the Muslim expansion outside of Arabia.

Aisha: One of the nine wives Muhammad married after Khadija's death, Aisha was said to be his favorite and the only one who had not previously been married. After Muhammad's death, she became a main source of information about him and his life. She threw her influential support on the side of the Umayyads during the Arabian civil war.

Ali: The son of Muhammad's uncle Abu Talib. Adopted by Muhammad, Ali became the first child to accept Islam and remained a loyal supporter all his life. He married Muhammad's daughter Fatima. For a brief time Ali was the fourth of the patriarchal caliphs.

al-Ma'moun: A caliph of the Abbasid dynasty from 813 to 833, he established the House of Wisdom and an astronomical observatory in Baghdad.

Abu Bakr Mohammad Ibn Zakariya al-Razi: Al-Razi was the greatest Muslim physician during the golden age. He wrote an encyclopedia of medicine and numerous other books, including a medical textbook, was the director of the leading hospital in Baghdad, and was the first person to distinguish between measles and smallpox.

Khadija: Muhammad's first wife, with whom he remained in a monogamous relationship for twenty-four years until her death. Khadija was Muhammad's greatest supporter and first believer. By all accounts they loved and cherished each other, and Muhammad never got over losing her.

Muhammad: Arab prophet and the founder of Islam. Muslims believe that Muhammad is the last prophet and the messenger of God.

Omar: The second of the patriarchal caliphs, Omar established the Islamic Empire in what Muslims view as wars of liberation in the territories surrounding Arabia, including a large part of the Persian Empire. He was an early convert to Islam and a close advisor to Muhammad, and during his caliphate he established the importance of following the Quran as the foundation of society and justice.

Umayyads: The second of the Islamic caliphates to rule after the death of Muhammad. The Umayyad dynasty ruled from 661 to 750 and established a vast empire, but their ascent to the caliphate caused the first rift in the Islamic world. Because of the secular nature of the Umayyad state, Muslims often refer to the dynasty as a kingdom instead of a caliphate.

Uthman: The third of the patriarchal caliphs, who expanded the Islamic Empire and oversaw the completion of a definitive written text of the Quran. Nevertheless, he was an unpopular ruler and the first to be assassinated by other Muslims.

For Further Research

Books

Sumbul Ali-Karamali, *Growing Up Muslim: Understanding the Beliefs and Practices of Islam*. New York: Delacorte, 2012.

Reza Aslan, *No God but God: The Origins and Evolution of Islam*. New York: Delacorte, 2011.

Bryn Barnard, *The Genius of Islam: How Muslims Made the Modern World*. New York: Knopf, 2011.

Sarah Conover, *Muhammad: The Story of a Prophet and Reformer*. Boston: Skinner House, 2013.

National Geographic, *1001 Inventions & Awesome Facts from Muslim Civilization*. Washington, DC: National Geographic Children's Books, 2012.

Omer, *Understanding the Basic Principles of Islam*. Clifton, NJ: Tughra, 2012.

Mardijah Aldrich Tarantino, *Marvellous Stories from the Life of Muhammad*. Markfield, Leicester, UK: Islamic Foundation, 2012.

Enis Yuce, *Companions of the Prophet*. Clifton, NJ: Tughra, 2011.

Websites

15 Famous Muslim (Arab & Persian) Scientists and Their Inventions, Famous Scientists (www.famousscientists.org/famous-muslim-arab-persian-scientists-and-their-inventions). This page lists fifteen Muslim scientists. Click an image to read a biography and a description of the scientist's achievements and contributions. Click the "Home" page to find a list of famous scientists around the world, including many Muslim ones.

History of Islam (http://historyofislam.com). This is an encyclopedia of Islamic history. Of particular interest is the section titled "Short Stories," which compiles several Muslim folktales and parables that illustrate morality and Muslim teachings.

Islamic Medicine on Line (www.islamicmedicine.org). At this large website, visitors can explore current Islamic medical philosophies, the history of Islamic medicine, and much more. To learn about the medical contributions during the rise of Islam, click the link titled "Muslims & Medical History" and follow one of the many recommended links.

IslamWeb (www.islamweb.net/emainpage). This site provides news and opinion pieces from an Islamic perspective and also has a section for kids. Click the link "Boys & Girls" to find interactive games, articles, and stories.

Muhammad FactCheck (www.muhammadfactcheck.org). The authors of this website dispute several claims about Muhammad and his teachings that are made by many historians. Visitors can read different views about, for example, whether Muhammad ordered Jewish tribes to be slain or whether he looted Meccan caravans.

Muhammad: Prophet of Islam (www.prophetofislam.com/index.php). This religious website offers facts about Muhammad from A to Z. Visitors can read chapters about what Muhammad said, what others say about him, and what Muslims today say about the Prophet.

Quran (http://quran.com). This website has translations of all 114 suras of the Quran. Visitors can read the different chapters separately or all the way through.

Religions, BBC (www.bbc.co.uk/religion/religions). A UK website that describes all the world's major religions in an easy-to-read way. The section on Islam describes its history as well as its beliefs.

Top 10 Most Beautiful Mosques in the World, Click Top 10 (www. clicktop10.com/2013/08/top-10-most-beautiful-mosques-in-the-world). This website offers photographs of mosques from places such as Spain, Russia, and Saudi Arabia. Each has a brief description with pertinent facts.

Index

Picture Credits

Scholars and astronomers in the observatory of Galata tower, Ottoman miniature, manuscript, Turkey,16th century/De Agostini Picture Library/G. Dagli Orti/The Bridgeman Art Library: 72

Page from the 'Canon of Medicine' by Avicenna (Ibn Sina) (980-1037) (vellum), Islamic School, (14th century)/National Museum, Damascus, Syria/The Bridgeman Art Library: 77

About the Author

Toney Allman holds degrees from Ohio State University and the University of Hawaii. She currently lives in Virginia, where she enjoys a rural lifestyle, as well as researching and writing about a variety of topics for students.